Charles, Sir Waldstein

The Jewish Question and the Mission of the Jews

Charles, Sir Waldstein

The Jewish Question and the Mission of the Jews

ISBN/EAN: 9783743311336

Manufactured in Europe, USA, Canada, Australia, Japa

Cover: Foto ©Thomas Meinert / pixelio.de

Manufactured and distributed by brebook publishing software
(www.brebook.com)

Charles, Sir Waldstein

The Jewish Question and the Mission of the Jews

CONTENTS

THE JEWISH QUESTION

Is there a Jewish Question at all ? I maintain that there is not, in the sense in which we speak of a Labour Question, or the Eastern Question, or the Home Rule Question. For the element of unity is lacking to the subject upon which it is proposed to establish a question ; and the attributes which it presents are different from, nay, opposed to, one another according to the circumstances in which it has been placed. So the Jews differ essentially from one another according to the nations among which they live and have lived for ages, the different classes to which they belong in these various communities, the several occupations they follow, and the tastes they possess. In political life they cannot be said to form one party, to give a distinct shading to any party, or to enable party politicians to appeal to them

A

as a body—and herein they differ from many of the other elements which make up the life of a colony or a younger state. For any practical purpose of political or social generalisation within the Occidental states and communities, the assumed unity of the Jews is an illusion; an illusion which tends to dim the sight even in those comparatively rare instances where those who would raise the question are not blinded by a definite animus.

Of late, attempts have been made to raise such a general question, or to set on foot so-called 'Anti-Semitic movements.' But they really are ridiculously unimportant when viewed in the light of the serious questions which move the main currents of modern history, and may stir humanity to the depths of its existence. They may no doubt be serious to many of the Jews themselves, causing them some annoyance for the time, if not deeper emotions, or even physical suffering. But they are artificial and false in their origin and ephemeral in their vitality, and they are doomed to die soon. One need but examine the existing movements in Russia, Germany, and France to see at once how little they have to do with what is essential to Judaism or the

Jews. The expulsion of the Jews from Russia —though no doubt religious superstition may have furnished an element of intensity to the spirit of persecution—emanates from a more positive source of Russian political life, namely, the consistent carrying out of what may be called a ' national ' policy. The watchword is ' Russia for the Russians.' And even the term Russian admits of various definitions, and may mean only those who conform in body, soul, and thought to the ruling powers of Russia at this present moment. Whatever class of men does not conform to the definition of Russian as held by those who now rule that country, is looked upon as a destructive growth upon the main stem of national life, and has to be extirpated and cast away— if such destruction and removal are possible. Siberia is the repository for the Russian subjects who manifest inconvenient political opinions. The dissentient Russians and the Poles are oppressed, and often expelled. If they dared, they would to-morrow expel all the Germans resident in Russia; and, should circumstances make it less dangerous, these would certainly be thus expelled—in fact, Russia would, if it could, and may some day expel

all foreigners of whatever nationality. I am
inclined to believe that of all foreign elements
in Russia the German residents, and those
of German origin, are most thoroughly hated
by the Russian people. To them would be
attributed, even more than to the Jews, the
charge of devouring the substance of the
people. But the Germans residing in Russia
have a powerful government at home with
whom the Russians must reckon; while the
Jews have no such potent protectors. So a
valiant, chivalrous autocracy finds it more
becoming to hurl its brutal force against the
Jews. The Jews, moreover, have been per-
manently established in the country, some of
them perhaps longer than many orthodox
Russian subjects; while the Germans in Russia
are professedly there as aliens, whose immediate
object is gain and nothing more. At all events,
the action of Russia has the advantage of a
consistent policy, and it is in keeping with an
autocracy which has never claimed to foster
freedom and to respect the rights of man. Nor
to my mind do the wrongs which it has inflicted upon the Jewish people compare in
proportion with those which they have suffered
at the hands of civilised society in other

European states. Look at the Anti-Semitic
parties in Germany and France, and the absurd
inconsistency will at once stare you in the face.
They present but a superficial, opportunist
movement with no real motive power. In
Germany they are now allied with the extreme conservative party, in France with the
ultra-radicals. The Prussian landowner is
afraid of a liberal movement which might lead
to the repeal of 'corn-laws.' This would take
from him the protection which he requires if
he is not to become bankrupt; and so he does
not hesitate to throw himself into the arms of
an Ahlwardt, a political adventurer who un-
furls the banner of anti-Semitism to fight the
battle of the conservative. On the other hand,
a small group of ultra-radicals in France raise
the anti-Semite's war-cry to fight the conser-
vatives. Finally, the Emperor of Russia is
dissatisfied with the socialistic and nihilistic
tendencies of the Jews. These phenomena
reveal the transparent insincerity, nay, the
childishness of these cries.

The anti-Semitic movements are only futile
attempts to delay, or to divert the course of, the
great and serious movements which threaten
to change the present state of our economic,

social, and political life.   If a Bismarck or the
Russian Czar, or a political adventurer cries
out, 'Here are the Jews, they are the bankers
and capitalists; why covet *our* money?' or,
'The Jews are at the bottom of modern socialistic theories and practices—repress them!'
that may for the moment satisfy the lower instincts of a vast number of people and lead to a
loud clamour—perhaps even to violent action;
but it will not help the solution of modern
economic problems.   Capital and Jew are not
synonymous terms, though there may be
several Jewish financiers like the Rothschilds;
nor are the Jews, as a race, the cause of the
socialistic movement, though Ferdinand Lasalle and Karl Marx, the intellectual founders
of the movement, were Jews.   There are pro-
portionately as many Jewish tradesmen and
bread-winners who aspire to become Rothschilds as there are non-Jewish bread-winners
of all persuasions and nationalities whose
aspirations lie in the same direction, and who
are equally remote from a full consummation
of these desires.   And there are in proportion
as many good Jewish *bourgeois* who fear the
red flag as there are Christian burghers who
fear socialism.   In my numerous wanderings

in different countries I have heard the most
contradictory grounds for anti-Semitic feeling,
all pointing to the greatest diversity of occupation and characteristics among the Jews;
now they are attacked because they follow
with so much success the ordinary and legitimate mercantile and industrial occupations,
now the professions of medicine and law, now
literature and journalism, now music; again
they fill the chairs of science in the German
universities, or even become leaders in European statesmanship. One may be opposed to
the German republicanism of Heine and Lasalle,
to the toryism of Disraeli, or to the patriotism
of Gambetta; but one cannot well be opposed
to the views of the one without approving of
the opposite views of the other—and they were
all Jews. I have still to learn that there is
anything inherently bad in the establishment
of factories and mercantile houses, in the vocation of a doctor, of a lawyer, of a man of science,
or letters, or art—nor even do I see anything
wrong in journalism as such. Where the
bitterness comes in is in the fact that success
creates jealousy, and that in all these walks of
life the Jews attain a high degree of excellence and prominence. I have, on several

occasions, heard anti-Semites summarise their vapid arguments by the naïve statement that the Jews were too superior for unprotected competition. But such jealousy is more readily accounted for than it is justified. Never yet in the world's history has excellence brought lasting discredit upon those who possess it. I am sufficiently optimistic and have enough faith in the good judgment of humanity (allowing it time) to believe that prominence in any legitimate sphere of life ultimately brings high esteem to the individuals or the social group possessed of it. At all events, in the saner and brighter chapters of the world's history excellence has not proved an undesirable quality.

No, the political palliatives will not stay the progress of disease. The mob to whom we may hurl the bone of 'Jewish capital' will not be kept from biting, and will not thus satisfy its hunger. Nay, this may merely whet its appetite and sharpen its teeth to attack the body to which this bone of capital belongs. The other bankers and capitalists, the *bourgeois*, the country squire, who call upon racial and religious prejudice and hatred in fear for their own safety, may find that their opponents cannot be deceived by such feeble duplicity. We may have little barbarous episodes of narrow vindictiveness and brutal passion; the scum of modern society will always be ready to join in the survival of that form of mediæval chivalry in which the knight, high astride on his trusty charger, secure in his coat of mail and chain armour, with long, well-poised lance, rode amongst a host of unarmed men, women, and children, and took their money as well as their lives. On the other hand, the educated radicals will remember from whom they got their teaching, and will know that their enemies cannot be classified by nationalities or fictitious races.

All these anti-Semitic movements will spend themselves in a short time. The cause of any immediate success that a party movement of this kind may have, lies in the nature of parliamentary government. It is due to the disproportionate strength and influence of a compact faction, however small, which holds the balance between two contending parties. Herein lies the deplorable strength of all 'faddist' movements. In a country that is governed by representative assemblies, if majorities are small, each of the two main parties has to count with any third party, however unimportant the inspiring idea, and however small the number of citizens which it contains. There is no idea, however ridiculous or immoral, which cannot claim some votaries ; and if these choose to band together and to form a party, they can gain a parliamentary power out of all proportion to their position in the nation. This is a problem and a difficulty in representative government with which wise men will have to grapple.

Besides these ephemeral 'movements' with which the Jews have to contend, there no doubt also exists a certain amount of permanent prejudice against them, generally among ignorant people. These people are ignorant of history, especially the history of the Jews, and are of that narrow, provincial cast of mind which requires some form of prejudice as its normal food. There are many people who must have somebody to be jealous of and to hate in order that they may preserve the normality of their generally-diseased emotional nature ; and though not all of these require the intensity of an individual object for this disapproval or hatred, there are but few who would forego the luxury of a 'pet aversion' expressed in the general terms of a social group or a nationality. National prejudices are natural to us so long as nationalities assert themselves; and I venture to say that every nationality becomes distasteful and offensive when it becomes obtrusive. This is especially the case when it is not focussed in the harmonious setting of its local surroundings, where it naturally becomes subordinated as a part of a complex and organic image with dramatic justification of its main characteristics.

To use a trite simile : Mutton and beef are good meat with each its own quality; but mutton which asserts its own flavour too strongly becomes 'sheepy,' and beef becomes 'beefy'—both offensive to the palate. Especially when seen in their own country, an Englishman, a Frenchman, a German, an Italian, or an American are fine types of humanity. But an Englishman (especially abroad) who continually causes the British lion to roar, who speaks of 'foreigners,' who asserts his national costume, manners, and habits in and out of place—a *John-bullying* Englishman can be very offensive. A very French Frenchman, who maintains the appearance and manner of his boulevards, *grasouilles* his r's in speaking of *gloire*, bows gracefully and says pretty things full of *esprit*, may be irritating if he be not amusing in a manner which he would resent were he conscious of the effect produced in others. We do not call this French, but Frenchy. A German who with tight trousers, generally angular clothes and manners, claps his heels together, raises his glass of beer or wine, and, in a military or would-be *bur-schikose* style, talks of the *Vaterland* and its glory, of German *Gemüthlichkeit* and *Treue*, produces an effect in which ungenuineness is mixed with coarseness. So with the Italian who gesticulates and rolls his eyes and reminds us, if not of the organ-grinder, at least of the *primo tenore* of a second-class opera; so, too, with the American, whether from the state of wooden nutmegs or from the far West, who constantly spreads the eagle and waves the Stars and Stripes, and with acrid nasality descants upon the advantages of elevators and ice-water, and whose manifest ideals are smartness or shrewdness and push. The offensiveness of such national characteristics will be admitted. But he who bases his general sympathy or antipathy upon such isolated instances or upon the caricatures he may have heard of or read of, without a deeper knowledge of the national life in its natural setting, without a wide experience of individuals typical of the nation, without some knowledge of the past history and the national genius of the people, will certainly lay himself open to a charge of folly; he betrays how unrefined is his sense of truthfulness, and is liable to grave moral reprehension for his hasty judgment.

Of course the Jews may manifest characteristics which are offensive. But I maintain that, owing to their past history, and their present dispersion and variety of occupation, they have fewer marked characteristics lending themselves to exaggeration than have the nationalities I have mentioned. Because the Jews are dispersed over the whole world, because of the prominent part they play in the history of modern civilisation, and because they have attributes and characteristics, real or imaginary, which make them distinguishable as a body, they are readily talked of as a unit, and, what is more, readily become as such an object of attraction or repulsion, love or hate—more readily, as things human go, of the latter. People in general are not over-conscientious about making assertions and generalisations. And the larger or more complex the body upon which they are passing judgment, the more readily do they appear to make up their minds. The less experience a person has of the world, the less he has travelled, the less he has really entered into the life of a foreign nation—in short, the less he knows of them, the more easily will he descant upon their strength and weakness, their virtues and vices. The young lady who has exchanged a few words with English-speaking waiters in Germany or France, and made some purchases in the shops, will tell you that the French are frivolous and immoral; the Germans, heavy, honest, but dull; the English, coarse and selfish; and the Italians, musical and passionate. Upon no group of human beings will most people feel it a duty to pass an opinion more readily than upon the Jew. 'I do not like the Jews,' they will tell you. 'The Jews only care for money.' They are 'ostentatious,' or 'greedy,' or 'revengeful,' or 'generally repulsive,' or whatever attribute most corresponds to the type which for the moment fills their narrow imagination; whether it be some character of fiction — Shylock, or the Wandering Jew,—or Judas Iscariot, or the Old-clothes Jew, whom they have some-time met or heard of. We do not only meet with such crude expressions of personal liking or dislike, but the opinion is often clad in the garb of well-matured and well-balanced thought and experience. It will be prefaced by ' You will always find that a Jew,' or 'Wherever they live.' The speaker will often venture upon the past history of these people, and may quote you a passage from Tacitus, or one of the Fathers of the Church, or Luther. If you are interested in this matter, or in truth, or in the methods by means of which people in general arrive at what they consider truth, test the case, and simply ask the person who thus generalises, how many Jews he has known intimately, or even superficially; and, with regard to the past history of this people, ask him anything about the fate and position of the Jews in the Middle Ages. I venture to predict, as has been my experience since this subject has interested me, that the result will be as invariable as it will be disastrous to the claims of such people to hold or express any opinion whatever on this question. You will in most cases find, first, that they have

known no Jew intimately, or that among their
intimate acquaintances, respected and often
admired by them, there were people of whose
Jewish origin they were not aware. You will
sometimes find that the generaliser himself
has, without knowing it, had Jewish ancestors;
and sad to say, with the most violent denun-
ciator you may find that he has had them, and
knows it. As regards the mere acquaintances,
you will find that his emphatic knowledge is
based upon a few business connections of
whose successes he may sometimes be envious.
He may have seen an Old-clothes Jew in the
street, or may have mistaken a poor man of some
other nationality for one. And as to the past
history of these people, you will find that even
those well-read in history, not excluding the
Jews themselves, are singularly ignorant of
the fate and history of the Jews since the
destruction of the Temple of Jerusalem.
Many a person, glowing with self-satisfaction
in the consciousness of his social advantages
and long pedigree, will stare in blank amaze-
ment and incredulity if you tell him that the
Jews, not to speak of the Biblical period, but
of modern times, may have had ancestors who
present a continuous chain of highly-civilised

units, conforming in every respect to the term 'gentlemen of culture,' during periods when the ancestors of most of the European nobles were revelling in coarseness, or ignorantly bending their backs to the command of their superiors. I have come to the conclusion that, though the modern prejudice is often influenced by envy and superstition, it is chiefly caused by ignorance of the actual state of the Jews in modern times and of their history in the past, and that this ignorance extends often to the most cultured Jews who are living among us. It will be my immediate aim to contribute to clearness in this matter; to fix and determine the Jewish question, to lay before the Jews as well as others some facts of which they may have been ignorant before, and, at all events, to put the main questions in such a form that people may be set to thinking seriously upon them.

Perhaps the strength and persistency of the Jewish people through these many centuries of suffering and martyrdom have lain in the fact that the national and religious characteristics were inseparably interwoven with one another. This blending of race and religion certainly constitutes the main difficulty in

B

arriving at a proper understanding of the
Jewish question in our time, and in fixing the
position which is to be given to the Jews, and
which they are to hold for themselves in the
social and political life of modern communities.
But in dealing with this question as regards
the immediate present and from a practical
point of view, it is absolutely necessary to
keep these two elements clearly separate.
The unjustifiable charges which are brought
against the Jews by their enemies are often
accompanied by a system of shiftiness. They
have been and are sometimes held up to popular hatred on a purely religious ground, for
being the cause of Christ's death, when really
the active opposition to them is one of race.
Again, we are distinctly informed by those
claiming the spirit of religious tolerance that
the objection to them is purely national, and
is founded upon difference of race, when really
it is based on a prejudice which penetrated
the mind with the earliest religious teaching,
and is maintained by the influence of sectarian
differences. In the same country we at one
time hear them charged with the love of
money, while on the other hand they are
reproved for filling the chairs of learning, and

crowding those literary and liberal professions, which have never been associated with the production of large incomes. Thrift, moderation, desire of self-improvement, intellectual acumen, industry and commercial ingenuity, which are commonly supposed to be social virtues, the reward of which is praise and distinction, are held up as reasons for censure and contempt when connected with this people. All these points it is our duty to face boldly and to see clearly.

The prominence which has been given to the question of race in connection with the opposition to the Jews is comparatively of recent date. It is the outcome of a movement which had its origin in Germany, being called forth by the definite political needs of that country, but which has had far-reaching and enduring effects (I believe for the bad), even after the immediate aim which evoked it had been fulfilled. As a reaction against the policy of Metternich, which consisted in neutralising the restless and revolutionary forces of the Austrian Empire by opposing different nationalities to one another, which would thus keep each other in check, the political unity of Germany was based upon the idea of a national

state; which state was to be the expression
of the unity of the people, a unity which was
supposed to be found in a common origin and
a common race. This idea of a common origin
was naturally used to kindle the national
enthusiasm of a people whose political weakness lay in the division into many petty states
and principalities. And thus, in connection
with the romantic spirit which reigned supreme
fifty years ago, yet with a correct political
instinct lying at the bottom of the artificial
and theatrical pose of the patriots of those
days, was developed the conception of a
pure German racial unity, as distinguished
from Romance and other enemies without.
This was used as the lever which was to move
all the separate blocks (smoothly polished
and floridly decorated marbles of prince-ridden
principalities, and clumsy unhewn stones
and rubble-stones of independent cities and
towns), from which was constructed the
huge edifice of the German Empire. The two
men who in modern times used this power
most effectually were Bismarck and Cavour.

It appears to me a blot upon modern German academic science, to which the world owes
so much, that, in the faculty of history and

political science, many academic leaders have
more or less consciously bent their science to
the service of current political views. Through
Germany and German historical science,
France, by reaction (maintaining the claims
of Romance nations), and by sympathy some
historians in England have followed in this
general retrograde movement towards the intensifying and stereotyping of the idea of the
national unit. The chief difficulty has arisen,
and most mischief has been done, through the
confusion of the terms *race* and *nation*. The
word which the German publicists have made,
National-Staat, must not be confused, as has
been and is so readily done, with the *Rassenstaat*. The *National-Staat* is one which, we
might say, has an historical unity, while the
Rassenstaat has an ethnological unity. Germany is at present a *National-Staat*; the
Austrian and Turkish empires are not; in them
the distinct and even opposed units of peoples
have remained distinct; they have no common
language, and they are fully conscious of the
separateness of their nationalities. But
national unity in this sense is not at all
identical with racial unity. The actual condition of the German people in our time, and

its history for the last centuries, distinctly confirm its claims to be a nation, or one people. History, language, and literature distinctly show this. To confirm this we need not go for support to the science of ethnology, which is much more likely, I may venture to say sure, to counteract the impression of such a unity; and, at all events, if we attempt to follow the attractions of this science, we may be led into many quagmires.

Ethnology is a most interesting scientific pursuit, but it is still in its infancy; and whatever claims to universal recognition its generalisations and hypotheses may have, it is quite premature and misleading as yet to bring them into anything like practical application. But this unwarrantable application has been and is being made every day whenever it suits a definite political party, or even private interests and purposes, with the idea or desire of invoking the aid of venerable science to objects that are far from being venerable in their character. It is then that unconsciously, or unperceived by those who are to be influenced, the idea of nation is merged into the idea of race. Then history is ignored in favour of a counterfeit ethnology; then it is

no more the Germany welded together by
common suffering, civilisation, literature, and
science since the Middle Ages, the Germany
of Lessing, of Goethe and Schiller, of Fichte, of
Heine; but a Germany of pure Germanenthum,
purely Teutonic, or, at all events, Aryan, with
which we have to do.   But the serious students
of ethnology and comparative philology themselves are becoming more and more cautious
of the distinctions and classifications that have
hitherto been current, and they all feel that
within the next few years there may be forth-
coming fundamentally different hypotheses,
even with regard to the broadest distinction of
human races.   At all events, it is absurd to
apply the results of this science to the practical
consideration of nations as they are now before
us.   I certainly venture to state that there is
not one country in the West of Europe which
on any hypothesis can claim purity of race
in the present day, or in any period of the
Middle Ages.   Who will tell what tribes
the people now dwelling in Germany are
made up of, since the barbarous hordes
(Huns, Goths, and Tartars) swept through
their country, and settled here and there, to
be followed in later centuries by invading

armies practising warfare in the spirit of
their time ? [1]

Travel through the German Empire from
north to south and east to west, mingle with
the crowds in the streets of the towns and
study the people in the country, and I venture
to say that if you could for a moment do away
with the similarity of dress and fashion, and
the manner of wearing beards, and the accidental habits of the present day which may
come from the school or the army, and if
you could ignore the fact that they all speak
the same modern German tongue, the idea of
racial unity among them would for ever be
destroyed in your mind. Nay, even as it is,
the lounger in the streets of Berlin may differ
as much from the Tyrolese mountaineers as he
does from the cockney of London, and their
speech may be almost as unintelligible to one
another. There is indeed an actual unity
among the people of Germany ; but this unity

[1] On the other hand, compare the pure 'Aryan,' the Indian,
even of the highest caste, with an ordinary European, as regards
colour and general physical appearance, and as regards his intellectual and moral habits of mind and life, and then compare the Western Jew (if you can always discern him) with
his Western fellow-countrymen of Christian persuasion, and
the absurdity of any such broad classification for practical
purposes will at once be evident.

is the modern summary of living conditions to which, in dying, the past ages have given their life, and has nothing to do with the Teutons, or the Hermonduri, or the Catts, or the Franks. The same is true of England, with its Picts and Scots, and Celts and Saxons, and Danes and Normans, and the immigration and assimilation of French, Dutch, German, Spanish, and Jewish elements. And so it is with France, and with Italy, and with Spain, and all Western European nations.

And now when we look at the Jews from the point of view of race and nationality, we find the same difficulty in arriving at a clear conception of unity which will serve any practical purpose and application in the present day. I will not go back to their early Biblical history. I will not dwell upon the question of their classification as a Semitic people, though, as Ranke puts it, their very existence and essential nature was not only in opposition and contradiction to the pagans of the classical world, but to the other Semitic powers then extant. Nor will I dwell upon the different elements, national and racial, which they assimilated many centuries ago, such as the kingdom of the Chazari, a warlike tribe that

became converted to Judaism; nor will I
dwell upon the distinctions drawn among
themselves in mediæval and modern times,
such as that of the Sephardi and the Ashkenazi. I will not even dwell upon the differences among them in the present day,
from the rough-and-ready aspects of manifest
ethnology; as when, taking the Polish Jews,
who present the greatest internal unity of
language and character, we are struck by the
large proportion of fair-haired and blue-eyed
men and women, who present a marked contrast to the black-haired and dark-eyed individuals, while both classes differ again from
others whose high cheek-bones and blond or
light-brown hair belong to the Slav type. I
will not dwell upon all that these points may
suggest; but, to bring the matter to a practical
head, I will take the case of a well-educated
modern Occidental Jew, one who is himself
born in Western Europe or America, of ancestors who, on the face of it, have for countless generations lived in the West.

Such a Jew, educated in an English, German, French, or American school and university, is certainly in looks, manners, character,
habits, tastes, and ideas as different from a

Jew of Turkey or Egypt or Russia as he can well be. The people to whom he corresponds in all essential points are the people of his own country in which he was born and bred and has lived. In this country, again, he will be more like a group of friends with whom he associates by natural social selection than like those with whom he does not associate. The difference between him and a Jew of essentially different occupations and social tastes will be as great as between an English university-man, of Christian persuasion, and a factory hand or farm labourer in the same country. He will certainly, as national distinctions now go, be more like the men following the same walk of life in his own country than he will be like those in Germany or France; and he certainly will be essentially different from the Jew of the East.

Now, what must such an Occidental Jew say of himself if he is true to himself, and if he recognises truth in all matters as the supreme guide of man? He will have to say that the strict racial unity of the Jews is doubtful, even with regard to the past; and as regards the present, he will have to deny it absolutely. Confirming his actual clear observation by the results of natural science—even with all due regard to Weissman's views—he would have to consider it nothing short of a miracle if, in his whole nature, he was not different from the dweller in the East.

He will have to retort to the anti-Semitic agitator that his ancestors probably lived in Germany and France before those of the persons who wish to claim supreme national rights on the ground of earliest settlement. Perhaps all the Jews of Germany have, in this respect, a greater claim to be considered Germans than men like Treitschke, whose name so evidently points to a Slav origin.

There certainly have been Jews in the North and South of Europe, and perhaps in England, in Roman times. There was an organised congregation at Cologne, probably in the third century A.D., while, not to mention the South of France and Spain prior to the Christian persecutions, the Jews were free occupants of the land all through the succeeding centuries; and, in spite of temporary expulsions and wholesale butcheries during the whole of the Middle Ages up to our own time, they at all times were dwellers in the West of Europe. So far as the physical con-

stitution of man is affected by climate and
soil, whether by the immediate influence of the
environment or by natural selection, these
Jews have become thoroughly occidentalised,
and as far as physical conditions are concerned,
they are under the same influences and have
been fashioned and affected in the same
manner as all the other peoples in Western
Europe from whom the citizens of the modern
Western nations spring.

Conscious of these facts with regard to his
physical history, the Occidental Jew of whom
I am speaking must furthermore not blind
himself to the elements which compose and
give their character to his intellectual and
moral nature. He must remain conscious, and
gratefully conscious, of the factors which
make up the civilisation in which he lives,
and which constitute the very core of his
inner existence during every day that he feels
or thinks or acts. It is difficult or impossible
to enumerate all these elements of modern
Occidental civilisation, but among them we
may single out a few. There is, first, the
element of Hebraism as it has filtered through
Western civilisation for so many centuries,
quite apart from the Hebraism inherent in

modern Judaism as it is handed down in the
worship and traditions of the living Jews of
to-day. Nor do I only mean the Hebraism as
it has passed through Christianity or Christian dogma, but I mean those fundamental
moral and spiritual ideas impersonated in the
history and, alas! the martyrdom of the Jewish people. This civilisation, which he shares
and to which he may contribute with all other
citizens of Western States, is also essentially
composed of and modified by the results of
the Renaissance, and the introduction of all we
mean by Hellenism, with regard to the fundamental fashioning of our taste—taste not only
for beauty in nature, in art and in literature,
but a quality of taste which directs the current
of our being and acting, and gives us our
delight in the acquisition of truth as a thing
to be admired, and of goodness that we worship
as a thing thoroughly harmonious, so that stern
effort and laborious duty are replaced by
admiration and worship. Nor must he ignore
the effect which the emphatic teaching of
Christian charity has had upon the formation
of the intellectual and moral ideals of man,
however much the treatment his ancestors may
have received at the hands of the Church and of

mobs of knights and serfs that marched under
its banner may have belied the tenets of Christ
in practice. He must also be aware of the wide
scope of vision which the intellectual development of Europe derived from the organisation
of the Catholic Church on the basis of the
Roman Empire. Furthermore, there is the
idea of chivalry in all its modified forms,
which at least adds its influence in making a
'gentleman,' and teaches him to do honour to
womanhood. He has also to share in the
stimulating influence of the Reformation, in
the levelling power of the invention of gun-
powder, in the untold benefits to intellectual
progress which the printing-press has given;
and he, too, has a part in the good results
which came from the terrible French Revolution. He must finally, above all, remember
his indebtedness to the moral standard of
modern times, that love of man as man which
is the result of no one of these currents alone,
but is the outcome of the action of all of them,
and to the standard of truth as intensified by
modern science.

Now, realising all this, he must admit that
a very small portion of his moral and intellectual existence is Jewish in the Orientalist

sense of the term, and he cannot thus be cramped back into the laws which are to govern the thought and life of a Jew as laid down in the Talmud and embraced by the practices of the devout and observant Jew. He is speaking and living a lie if he denies this by word or deed; and those who by word or deed deny him the right of being in every sense a full Occidental citizen speak and live a lie. Yet this lie is lived by many Jews of superior moral and intellectual quality, generally from the mistaken sense of chivalry. Put yourself in the place of such a Jew. He lives among traditions that have a deep poetry from their age, from the centuries during which they have retained their influence, corresponding to the poetry which presents itself to one who looks back upon a long line of ancestors. He feels strongly what the Jews have always retained (and may they ever do so and teach it to others), the family piety which makes each successive son shrink from denying the love which his father manifests to him in life or which still lives in his memory. The desire not to grieve by any act of dissent those who are nearest to him is a strong one. And, above all, he feels the spirit of chivalry, or

call it pluck; for he sees those of his own
descent suffering, if not the rack and the
fagot, still from the slings and arrows which a
cruel society can wield, and he knows that
the wounds they cause are none the less
painful that they are inflicted in ignorance.
He realises with contempt how many in times
of tribulation have been renegades, and what
harm they have done; not only by the slur
they thus cast upon their people, but by the
fact that they have generally been possessed
of wealth or of superior intellectual power,
and their success in the world of thought or
action has been lost to the estimation which
could be formed of the whole people. He
must feel himself a coward if he denies them
so long as they are in adversity. He can, in
his mind, live through the struggles which
such a great and noble soul as Spinoza must
have gone through: he can realise what moral
courage it required for him to follow the
stern summons of truth, and to leave his
own people in misery. And he cries out,
as the Psalmist of old: 'If I forget thee,
O Jerusalem, let my right hand forget her
cunning. If I do not remember thee, let
my tongue cling to the roof of my mouth;

if I prefer not Jerusalem above my chief joy.'

And what is the result ? There remains an unreal and artificial unity, which neither raises the members of the society themselves, nor allows the good they may have to teach to penetrate readily into the other circles among which they live. And as there is not a free differentiation in which, without violence or unfriendliness, the groups of natural affinity form themselves and become organised in free social intercourse, and as distinctions are not made among themselves, it is but natural that others should not distinguish between the good and the bad, the cultivated and the unculti-vated. And if a private insult is offered to one member of this varied body, it is looked upon by some as an insult to the whole race. We get, moreover, the manifest ab-surdity that, while they still profess, and in part act up to, the belief in this un-real unity, they, on the other hand, consider it a great injustice if a bad, or even a good, man among them is denoted or char-acterised and distinguished by the terms of a racial difference, which on every side they fictitiously claim. The result of meeting with prejudices, and even persecution, seems to me inevitable.

It appears to me to be almost an historical law, that wherever there is a distinct community, or class within the community, it sooner or later becomes the object of hatred, contempt, or persecution. Look to any country and you will find that if there be a body of settlers or emigrants who, from the fact of living together, or by pronounced distinctive traits, become readily noticeable as a distinct class, they will necessarily take a secondary social position (unless they are conquerors in the bloody or unbloody warfare), and this secondary position will in due course produce contempt, and may further lead to persecution. The feelings of envy and jealousy are unfortunately so thoroughly engrained in human nature, that if success in the acquisition of what is generally admitted to be desirable comes to such distinctive bodies, or to individual members among them, the feeling of the masses, and, unfortunately, even of the more highly educated, rises against them. This is so not only with the Germans in England and France, but even with the German settlements in the provinces of Austria and

Hungary, where the term 'Schwab,' standing
for all Germans, is one of derogation. This
is so with the Italians and the French, and
would be so with the English if their colonies
did not form such a natural and attractive
outlet for their surplus emigration. The success of foreign bodies in commerce and finance
evokes envy, not only against the Jews, but
against any other body that may thus manifest itself in its solidarity. George Meredith,
in his latest novel, *One of Our Conquerors*,
illustrates this by sentiments that he puts into
the mouth of a London city philosopher who
fears for the repression of the Saxon race:
' Hengist and Horsa, our fishy Saxon originals,
in modern garb, the liverymen and gaitered
squire, flat-headed, paunchy, assiduously servile, are shown blacking Ben Israel's boots
and grooming the princely stud of the Jew.
. . . Including the dreaded Scotchman as well,
and Americans and Armenians and Greeks:
latterly Germans hardly less.' If this social
law be, as I hold it to be, true, then, especially
considering the crass ignorance that prevails
concerning the history of the modern Jew, it
is not to be wondered at if wholesale charges
are brought against him, such as his well-

known money greed (which, as I shall show, is absolutely unfounded as regards this people), or his parasitic nature, or any other attribute that may express the envy which the less successful of every class feel against their happier fellow-citizens.

Recognising the evils of racial exclusiveness, what ought such a modern Occidental Jew to do? He has simply to live up to his convictions in every detail of his life. He must not only, as he has ever done, perform the duties of a citizen in the country in which he lives, fully and conscientiously, but he must refuse, as far as the race question goes, in any way to recognise the separate claims of the Jews within his country. As a matter which concerns his own inner consciousness, and, if provoked by assertion in others, he may feel justly proud of being a descendant of a race which is not only the oldest and purest, but has through many centuries steadfastly followed the guidance of a great spiritual idea to the blessing of mankind, just as a Norman or a Saxon or a Celt in Great Britain may, when called upon to do so, consider, and be gratified by, the memory of his own racial origin. Beyond this he must not go. He must spurn and avoid all

those symbols and rites which have been established to signify a separate, even though a
chosen, people. His marriage and his choice
of friends must be exclusively guided by those
considerations of inner affinity which are
likely to make such unions perfect as far as
things human can be perfect. His business
and social relations must be entirely free from,
and unbiassed by, any considerations of the
relationship of race, and he must no more
admit into his circle of intimate friends a
person of Jewish origin, because of his origin,
than he would shut him out on that account.
He must, in one word, as I have said before,
keep his life from being a lie, and live up to,
in every respect, what he considers truth.

There may be some complicated cases, such,
for instance, as is presented by the question,
What must the attitude of a Jew be towards
the Russian Jews who are undergoing so hard
a fate? Well, then, so long as he does not
look upon them as religious fellow-worshippers
(which may certainly be a tie, such as a
Churchman or a Wesleyan would feel towards
his foreign co-religionists), he must be actuated
by simple motives of humanitarianism. He
must feel for the oppressed, as we should all

feel for an Indian or an Armenian or a Bulgarian or a negro slave ; the only difference is that there are greater ties of piety binding the Russian Jews to all of us, Jews and Christians alike ; as regards the Western Jew, there is a certain relationship of race to be traced many centuries back ; and, as regards the Christian, he should not forget that the human sojourn and nationality of his Lord was among the ancestors of these people, that it is out of them that the Christian religion has arisen, and that their national documents are included among its sacred writings.

But if this Occidental Jew should feel the element of race and its claims more strongly than I have put them, then there is but the other alternative, that he and they must strive to form a Jewish state. No race has a right to separate existence without a state ; though we must carefully guard against assuming the converse to be true, namely, that no state can exist without a unity of race. This was felt even by one of their greatest men, during the flower of culture of their life in Spain in the tenth century, Chasdai Ben-Isaac Ibn Shaprut, who was overjoyed to hear of the Jewish kingdom of the Chasari. It has been one of the glories of the Jews on the religious and moral side, and has, I strongly believe, been to the benefit of the world at large, that they should have survived through all the adversities and persecutions, keeping their faith and their God undefiled. For this they have suffered the great martyrdom of centuries, and the world ought to be grateful to them for it. But at the same time it was the cause of their own misfortune ; it was, if I am not misunderstood in saying so, an historical crime that they should have maintained the mock unity of race after the people as a people and as a nation had gone. If it is strongly felt that this unity of race ought to be preserved, then we must do all in our power to make the Jews a nation or state. In pondering much upon this subject I at one time thought it not only desirable, but even thoroughly practicable. By this I did not mean that all the Jews scattered throughout the world were to leave their actual homes and to settle in this newly-founded state ; this would be as little necessary as it is that all Englishmen should crowd together in the British Isles. But I hold, as I shall show, that the Jew's ideal mission to the world has been and is being fulfilled in the manner in which they are now dispersed over the earth ; and I do not feel convinced that the foundation of such a state is necessary or most desirable.

The attitude and action of such a modern Occidental Jew with regard to the question of race and nationality seems to be clearly defined. But if such a Jew believe in the Jewish Church, what, then, is to be his attitude and his life ? Here again we are met with countless difficulties, which stand in the way of a clear conception of the case ; difficulties which I feel convinced neither the Jews themselves nor those who have thought or spoken about them have dared to face and to dissolve into their constituent factors. For the first question we are met with is one concerning the unity of the Jewish faith, or the Jewish Church. And it appears to me that the history of Judaism in the past centuries, as well as the state of their religion in the present, does not warrant us in calling it a unity. There are in the past and in the present among the Jewish sects differences of doctrine and of ritual which are as great, if not greater, than those which separate the Church of Rome from the numerous Protestant sects. When making this remark, I have been often told that the unity of the Church and the essential features of the Jewish religion were to be found in pure monotheism. If this be so, I must still urge the central question, which the thoughtful Jew must ask himself and answer clearly and unequivocally : Do you believe in Jewish theism as restrictedly national, or as simply a spiritual belief in one God first recognised by the Jews ? The unenlightened Jew may at once answer : 'My faith is distinctly national ; I cannot conceive a God or pray to Him without the admixture of a Hebrew prerogative.' Well, then, the religion of such a one is essentially, not accidentally, different from the faith of him who may be called an Occidental monotheist. But the Jew who knows of no such national restriction to his theism will furthermore have to face the proposition that no man can consider himself as being of the Jewish faith who does not believe in the direct inspiration of the Old Testament by God as a book intrinsically holy, not by its tradition only ; who does not believe in the exceptionally holy character of the Talmud, perhaps even of the Cabala, just as no man can be called a Christian who does not believe in the divinity of

Christ and in the exceptionally holy character of the Old and New Testaments. The Occidental Jew who does not believe in this, and whose theism is not restrictedly national, may refer in piety to the past of the Jewish people, but he must consider himself an Occidental theist or deist, such as Locke and many others have been. This Occidental monotheist is truer to his own intellectual development, for pure Judaism has to a great extent kept itself free from those Occidental elements which I have enumerated above as forming part of the moral and intellectual consciousness of the Western Jew. He must choose whatever contemporary form of thought corresponds most fully to his own belief.

Yet I can well understand how difficult it will be for one brought up in the Jewish faith and imbued with the heroic grandeur of Jewish history to accept this readily. The influence of piety to which I have alluded with regard to race may even at this point urge its claims more strongly. He will be justified in saying, 'Why should not the religious theist, the Unitarian, and all members of similar sects, come over to us and become reformed Jews? In the past centuries, when our faith in its outer form differed more essentially from the current beliefs, and admission into our national body constituted a much greater change than it now would, there have been priests and laymen who faced the danger and underwent the fate of martyrdom at the stake, and became converted to Judaism. If our faith is essentially the same as theirs, then we have in addition the poetry and inspiring grandeur of a beautiful and continuous history; for our faith the blood of martyrs has been shed, it is mellowed by centuries of endurance and the memory of unparalleled steadfastness under tribulation. We have the hoariness and venerableness of age, so important in the poetry and sentiment of faith; we have nurtured in us the flame kept alive by the first breath of countless new-born babes and by the last gasp of millions of dying men and women. We are the parent of Christianity; in our faith the Christian Lord was reared as a man. Is all this to be swept away? Why not come to us, and now that the period of physical martyrdom has gone by and the sun smiles, why should the night of extinction be spread over all?' Who could be deaf to the poetry and justice of such a plea?

There is a way of responding to these just
demands and at the same time corresponding
to truth and fact. This lies in the establishment of a Neo-Mosaic Church. I say Mosaic,
and not Judaic or Hebraic. The racial
element is to be excluded; while it is to
comprise all those who believe in the pure
monotheism, which was first given to the
world by Moses, together with those laws of
morality out of which our highest conceptions
of right and wrong have been evolved.
Account will thus be taken of the actual
history of monotheistic belief; while the
poetic inspiration, the vivid and vital life of
ages handed on continuously to the future, the
piety for the past and for all that has withstood
the test of stormy times—elements so important in any living religion—will increase the
vitality and reality of such a Church without
impairing and hampering the clearest expression of its articles of faith. The ritual may be
based upon the ritual of the Jewish Church to
any degree compatible with the unequivocal
expression of faith and the refusal to acknow-
ledge any narrow racial limits. The language
is to be only that of the country in which the
Church finds itself; for, as a mediæval Jewish

rabbi said, one cannot pray without understanding the language in which the prayer is couched. The elements of ethical and religious teaching which have become the property of civilised nations through the Middle Ages and modern times, including those in the New Testament—for instance, the sayings of Christ, in so far as they do not clash with pure monotheism—will have to be assimilated. The teaching will thus be the nearest to that of a large portion of the Unitarian Church and of advanced sections of other Churches. But it will add to these the historical background of a continuous development of monotheistic beliefs for several thousand years. It is, in fact, the only Church to which most Unitarians can consistently belong.

I have hitherto spoken chiefly of one type of Jew, namely, the purely Occidental Jew, in whom Occidental culture has been an essential element. But there are numerous gradations of Jews;—as for that, there are numerous gradations among all bodies of men. One of the many errors we wish to combat is the slip-shod and untrue classification of all these people, so diversified among themselves, as a definite unit.

There is, therefore, an imperious necessity presenting itself to the Jews themselves and to those who deal with them or the Jewish question, namely, the necessity of differentiation, if not of disintegration.

For the class we have been dealing with, namely, those of European antecedents and habits, the separate existence of a Jewish race is untrue, and is an evil. It only exists historically as an element of poetic pride and inspiration. With regard to religion, they will naturally turn towards theism, especially that form which I have just suggested in the Neo-Mosaic Church. But they will always have to be tolerant of, and even sympathetic towards, their brethren, to whom this form is too narrow or too wide, and who truthfully live up to their inner convictions.

We next have those who, while also Occidental and European, still cannot, or will not, dissociate their monotheism from the actual Jewish people and their past history. These will be (as their religion in its essential teaching enjoins, and as they have always been) good citizens in the countries in which they live. They will thus have every claim to political freedom and equality, and to all

privileges of citizenship ; they will meet with
the tolerance and sympathy with regard to
their religious views which all enlightened
people grant to every faith truly held.   But,
being thus manifestly recognisable as a distinct body within the general community,
they must not be astonished or aggrieved if
they are spoken of as a body or class, and meet
with expressions of approval or disapproval
as a body.   But they will be justified in claiming that such generalisations be based upon
knowledge of facts, and correspond to truth,
and are not, as is generally the case, the result
of ignorance and jealousy.   Just as any Scotch
or German community within an English district, manifesting itself in any way as a body,
might be considered as a body, though they,
too, can claim truth and justice.

Finally, should there be among us those who
are not essentially European, more Jewish
than Occidental, with no tendency towards
assimilation into the main body of the people
among whom they live (if such there be), these
must submit to be treated as aliens, as aliens
are treated in civilised states.   The ideal for
these, as for all who cling to racial distinction,
is the formation of a Jewish state.   To such a

Jewish state would belong the task of carrying into the East the civilisation of the West ; as in the Middle Ages their forefathers brought among the barbarians of the West the torch of culture, which had been kept alight by them in their journey from the East.

To all Jews alike we owe a kindly reverence and sympathy for the maintenance of a faith which is of such antiquity, and has been tested by such trials. For what is the martyrdom of Christianity in its early days, or of one or other of its forms during a definite historical period, compared to the continuous martyrdom of the Jews during so many centuries? The day will have to come, and will come, when all people will join in erecting a monument to the Jewish martyrs.

II

THE MISSION OF THE JEWS

In the first half of the first century A.D. there lived in Alexandria the philosopher Philo. He was born about the year 20 B.C., and died about the year 55 A.D. He belonged to one of the wealthiest and most distinguished families in the East, being brother to Alexander the Arabarch—that is, the ruler over the Arabic and Jewish portion of the inhabitants of Alexandria. He was also connected with influential people in the Roman empire, and with the family of the King of Judah, whose beautiful daughter Berenice was at first betrothed to his brother's son Marcus. But his distinction did not rest upon the brilliant social conditions into which he was born, nor even upon the prominent political position he held; though he was selected as one of the ambassadors who was sent to Rome to shake the resolution of

the Emperor Caligula to cause his own statue
to be erected in the synagogues.   The respect in which Philo was held in his own
time, and the admiration which posterity has
for him, is based upon the lofty purity of
his character and upon the depth and beauty
of his numerous writings.   He had, as had
many of the Hellenic Jews of that period,
been thoroughly trained in all the arts and
sciences which then found their home in
Alexandria.   He was well versed in grammar,
rhetoric, music ; he had not only studied all
the treasures of Greek literature, and the
physical and mathematical sciences, but he
had mastered the works of the great philosophers and their schools ; Plato became so
thoroughly his favourite that a later authority,
Suidas, in an exaggerated epigram speaks
of Philo as platonising or Plato as philonising.
He also felt himself closely related to the
Stoic school of philosophy because of the lofty
moral tone which pervaded its ethical system ;
as, for the same reason, he felt himself strongly
opposed to the Epicurean philosophy, which
seemed to him to favour more the sensual life
of the Greeks he saw about him.   He thus
was one of the most prominent precursors of

the Neo-Platonic school of Greek philosophy, and one of the ornaments of the Hellenic literature of his period.

But besides these elements, in this rich nature there was another side to the great man, the most prominent one, namely, the Hebrew side. He was in his heart and in his life a true Jew, ever loyal to his people, and ready to sacrifice his blood for them; the chief inspiration of his intellectual and moral existence he derived from the Mosaic laws and the writings of the Prophets. In all his philosophical and metaphysical disquisitions the predominant chord is the pure monotheism revealed to the world through the means of his people. This it is which underlays the mystery of the world's creation and preservation. And in all his lofty speculations upon the ideals of a pure and noble life, he found the moral laws governing the Jewish people to be the ultimate and safest guides.

These two elements in the man, who was at once Greek and Jew, are also the two marked features in all his writings—Hellenism and Hebraism. And, as in his life and in his character, he endeavoured to reconcile and to fuse into one these two contending forces,

which, like the parties in his own city of
Alexandria, were at enmity with one another,
so in his writings we see a perhaps futile
attempt at reconciling these two leading currents of thought. Towards the harmonising
of Hellenism and Hebraism the greatest men
of these many succeeding centuries have been
working, until perhaps only in our time a final
fusion may be hoped for. For, as Heine has
said :—

> 'The contrasts here discordantly are paired,
> The Greek's delight, Judæa's thought of God.
>
> .   .   .   .
>
> Oh, never more will ended be this strife,
> And truth will war with beauty evermore.'

We need not be astonished to find that Philo
failed to reconcile the two in his philosophical
system ; nor, considering the wave of mysticism
which spread over the whole intellectual life
of that period, should we be repelled by the
frequent licence in the application of allegory,
which led him often to distort the plain meaning of Scripture in order to see embodied in
it, and anticipated by it, all the results of
Greek thought and metaphysics. With all the
Hellenic beauty and depth of thought which
are to be found in his numerous writings, we

constantly feel that the Mosaic teachings gave
the first impulse, as their confirmation seems
to be the ultimate result.   He is chiefly moved
by the practical effects of this teaching upon
the formation of his own soul in its appreciation of right and wrong, and by the manifest
effect it appears to have had upon the
Jewish people as shown in the contrast of
their life with the dissoluteness of the Greeks
he saw about him.

The documents of Judaism, according to
him, contain the deepest wisdom; what the
greatest philosophers among the Greeks only
taught to their select disciples, the whole of
the Judaic people draw out of the laws and
customs known to them all, especially the
knowledge of the one Eternal God (casting
aside all the vain and deceptive gods) and
the duty of kindness and humanity towards
all creatures. 'Are not these laws,' he says,
in one of his books (*De Septenario XII.*),
'worthy of being revered by all? They teach
the rich to give part of their riches to the poor,
to console the unfortunate; they ordain that a
time should come in which the poor need not
knock at the doors of the rich, but will receive
their possession again; for in every seventh

year the widows and orphans, and all who are disowned, shall once again come into wealth.'

The highest virtue, according to him, contains two main duties: the worship of God, and love and justice to all men. In the Mosaic laws he sees five chief points: first, that there is but one God; then, the unity of that Godhead (as opposed to those philosophers who assumed a dualism of contending forces); then, that the world was created by God; further, that there is but one world; and, finally, that this world is directed in its course by the providence of God. In answer to the attacks of the Pagans, he compares the written and unwritten laws of Judaism with the moral standards that govern the heathens. At the head of all these unwritten laws he places Rabbi Hillel's golden words: 'What thou dislikest that do not unto others.' Judaism, he says, does not only condemn the refusal of fire and water to those who want it, but it lays positive injunctions upon all to give to the poor and the weak what they require for life; it distinctly forbids the use of false measures and false money; it forbids the separation of children from their parents, of the wife from her husband, even if they are lawfully bought as slaves; it also enjoins the duty of compassion towards animals. He then defends the Sabbath against the attacks of such writers as Lysimachus and Apion. The Jews, he says, are able during one day in seven to become acquainted with their laws through reading and interpretation, and they are all saved from ignorance. The husband can teach the wife, the father the child, and the master the slave, so that all are capable of giving an account of the laws. It is, he says, the object of the Sabbatical year not only to give a periodical rest to the land which requires it, but also to give to those who have no such possessions an opportunity of gathering the fruits, for the law of property is suspended in that year.

Of the mission of the Jews themselves, and of their position in the world, Philo has the loftiest and most ideal conception. Although heaven and earth belong to God, He has elected the Jewish people as His chosen people, and destined it to His service as the eternal source of all virtues. The Israelites have, in his opinion, laid upon them the great task of serving for the whole race of men as priests and prophets; of opening out to them the truth, and, more especially, the pure knowledge of God. And therefore the Jewish people enjoy the special grace of God, who will never withdraw His hand from them. Compared to other nations, he continues, the Jewish nation appears like an orphan. Other nations assist one another; they, isolated by their own laws, can never count upon such assistance. For this very severity of the Judaic laws, which is necessary to the attainment of the highest degree of virtue, repels the other nations that are given over to a life of pleasure-seeking. But just because of the orphanage and desolation of this people can they hope for the mercy of God. Philo was thoroughly imbued with the belief that the dispersed and suffering Israelites would once, through the intervention of the Messiah, be collected together and led home, where the grace of God would again turn upon them and shine upon them, and they would be rewarded for their endless suffering and their prolonged steadfastness. The symbol of this nation of priests he held to be the flowering almond staff of Aaron, which indicates that they will always retain budding vitality and will enjoy eternal springtide.

Just about a thousand years after Philo was

born in Alexandria—about the year 1086—
there was born in Castile in Spain, where the
Jews formed a great centre of a prosperous
and highly-cultivated life, a youth whose name
was Abulhassan-Yehuda-Ben-Samuel-Halevi,
and is commonly known to posterity under the
name of Yehuda-Ben-Halevi. He became one
of a succession of great poets, two of the chief
names among which were his predecessors, Ibn
Esra (Abu Harun Mose, born about 1070, and
died about 1139) and, of a still earlier date,
Ibn Gebirol, of Malaga (born about 1021, died
1050). He attended the School of Alfassi, at
Lucena, because in Castile and the north of
Spain there were not celebrated authorities in
Talmudic teaching. While still a boy he
devoted much time to his Hebrew, rabbinic
studies, and to the science which subsequently
made him a skilled physician, while he widened
the sphere of his learning by becoming a
thorough master also of the Arabic and Castilian tongues, and penetrated deeply into the
study of ancient philosophy. But it was the
lyric muse which chiefly held his heart and
mind ; and from his earliest years he began
to write verses in Hebrew, Arabic, and Spanish.
His earliest poems strike a lighter strain. In

the most beautiful form they deal with the joys of life and love and wine. Above all, it was the beauty of nature which inspired him to burst forth in melodious verse.

But in his full development he betook unto himself one bride, and remained true to her through all hardships and sufferings to the end of his days. This bride was Jerusalem. So strongly did he feel the attraction which this local embodiment of his own people exerted upon him, that in misfortune and weak in health he undertook the pilgrimage to Jerusalem, and ended his eventful life in the East, never returning to his own native home.

Heine, who has devoted to him a long poem, and was capable of appreciating the beauty of these Hebrew verses, gives a most adequate account of this noble singer:

' Ah ! he was the greatest poet,
Torch and starlight to his age,
Beacon-light unto his people ;—
Such a mighty and a wondrous

Pillar of poetic fire
Led the caravan of sorrow
Of his people Israel
Through the desert of their exile.

Pure and truthful, fair and blameless,
Was his song, and thus his soul was.
When the Lord that soul created,
With great joy His work beheld He,

And He kissed that soul of beauty.
Of His kiss the fair faint echo
Thrills through each song of Halevi,
By the Lord's grace sanctified.

As in life, so in our singing,
Highest gift of all is grace—
Holding this, he never falters,
Not in prose nor yet in verses.

Such we call a genius,
By the grace of God a poet :
Irresponsible his kingdom,
O'er the thought-world ruling, reigning,

Gives account but to the Godhead,
Not the people ; for in art-work
As in life the people can but
Slay, yet never can they judge us.

. . . . .

And the hero whom we sing of,
He, Yehuda Ben Halevi,
Had of all one lady chosen—
Yet she was of different moulding.

She was not a favoured Laura,
Whose fair eyes, mere mortal starlight,
In the duomo on Good Friday
Spread the famous conflagration.

Nor was she a *chatelaine*
Who presided at the tourneys
In her flower of youth and beauty,
And distributed the laurel.

No fair barrister of kiss-right
Was she, not a wise professor
Who did lecture in the college
Of a court of love right wisely—

She, the fair love of the rabbi,
Was a poor and saddened sweetheart,
Was destruction's woful image
And was named Jerusalem.'

While at Granada he practised the profession of medicine to provide for his livelihood; yet all his spare time was devoted to the writing of masterpieces of poetry in the three languages to which he has added jewels. But his longest and greatest poems, dealing with the subject that was ever nearest to his heart —his own belief and his own people—were written in Hebrew. The climax of his poetic production is the poem called 'Chozari.' In the form of this poem he seems to have been influenced chiefly by the author of the Book of Job, and by the Platonic Dialogues; for it is in the more dramatic scheme of dialogue that he gives expression to these his loftiest views.

He takes the pagan prince, who feels a great
thirst for religious knowledge, and before
slaking it at one of the three great sources—
Judaism, Christianity, or Mohammedanism—
wishes to examine the three severally.   The
essential features of these three beliefs are
laid before him, and he chooses Judaism.
The poem is throughout a glorification of the
Hebrew faith, but it also contains a lofty conception of the mission of the Jewish people.

The degraded form of slavery which Israel
has assumed in its exile among the peoples is
to his mind no proof of its degeneration and no
cause for hopelessness as to the future, as little
as the spread of power which Christianity
and Mohammedanism can display is proof of
the divinity in the teaching of either. Poverty
and misery, which are the causes of contempt
in the eyes of man, stand higher in the eyes of
God than greatness and pride.   While the
Christians are not proud of those who hold
worldly power among them, they do glory in
the martyrs, above all in Christ, who enjoined
upon His followers that they should offer the
left cheek to him who strikes the right, and
they are proud of their Apostles who, humbled
and despised, suffered martyrdom.   So, also,

the Mohammedans pride themselves upon the assistants of their prophet, who suffered much sorrow on his account.

But the greatest of all sufferers is Israel, because it is to mankind what the heart is to the human organism. As the heart is affected by all ailments of the body, so the Jewish nation is at once smitten by every misfortune which designedly or unwittingly emanates from the people. To Israel the word of the prophet applies when he makes the people of the earth say, 'Surely He has borne our griefs and carried our sorrows.' But in spite of its unspeakable misery the Jewish people has not died away, but is rather like unto one who is dangerously ill, on whom the art of the physician has lost its effect, but who expects his recovery from a miracle. To Israel the figure of the prophet Ezekiel of the vision of the dry bones applies when he says : 'So I prophesied as I was commanded; and as I prophesied, there was a noise, and behold a shaking, and the bones came together, bone to his bone. And when I beheld, lo, the sinews and the flesh came up upon them, and the skin covered them above ; but there was no breath in them. Then said He unto me, Prophesy unto the wind, prophesy, son of man, and say to the wind, "Thus saith the Lord God; Come from the four winds, O breath, and breathe upon these slain, that they may live." So I prophesied as He commanded me, and the breath came into them, and they lived, and stood up upon their feet, an exceeding great army.'

All this is Israel in its present form of misery. It was by the wondrous design of Providence that the people of Israel was dispersed over the world, in order that it might penetrate with its spirit the whole of humanity. The race of Israel is like seed-corn that is laid into the earth and for a time vanishes from the sight of man, appears dissolved into the elements of its surroundings, and retains no trace of its original essence; but then when it begins to sprout and grow, it again assumes its original nature, the disfiguring shells are thrown off, and it purifies the elements, transforming them according to its own essence, until step by step it leads them to higher growth. When once the race of men, prepared by Christianity and Islam, recognise the true destiny of the Jewish nation as the bearer of divine light, they will honour the root upon which formerly they looked with contempt; they will grow more closely to it and will become purified fruit, and will enter into the Messianic kingdom, which is the fruit of the tree.

Eight hundred years after Yehuda-Ben-Halevi lived, suffered, and sang, there arose another man whose soul also was filled with the heavenly light of poetic fire. It was Heinrich Heine, born at Düsseldorf in 1799, died in Paris, 1856. He was endowed with poetic genius as only few have ever been. Both with regard to his poetry and his prose writings his must be classed among the very first names of Germany. But in the manifestations of character in his life he does not represent the purity and grandeur of the two great Jews whose conception of the Jewish mission we have just mentioned. Yet, in judging this great man, one will always have to consider how far his own morbid sense of self-depreciation and the paradoxical obtrusion of his own faults give a true picture for the estimation of his life and character; and one will also have to bear in mind the general tone and fashion of frivolity or dissoluteness which

E

characterised the romantic period in which he
lived, and which attaches to the personality of
most of the poets of that age. He did not
remain true to Judaism, and in the year 1825,
after some protest, he was baptized into the
Christian Church. But towards the close of
his life the spirit of levity seems to have left
him, and with it there came a glowing penetra-
tion into the depths of his native belief. For
once he seems to have thrown off entirely the
satirical faun's mask with which he was wont
to cover and hide his true features. There is
a truth and depth in the tone of his confession
with regard to Judaism which one never meets
with in all his other writings, and he thus
bursts into a thrilling panegyric on the Old
Testament. 'The Jews,' he says, 'ought to
console themselves that they have lost Jerusalem and the ark ; such a loss is but trifling in
comparison with the Bible, the indestructible
treasure which they have saved. The regen-
eration of my religious feeling I owe to this
holy book, and it became to me as well a source
of salvation as an object of the most glowing
admiration. I had not been particularly fond
of Moses formerly, perhaps because the Hellenic spirit was predominant in me, and I could

not forgive the legislator of the Jews his
hatred towards all sensuous form. I did not
see that Moses, in spite of his attacks upon
art, was still himself a great artist. Only his
artist's spirit, as with his Egyptian countrymen, was turned towards the colossal and indestructible. He builded pyramids of humanity (*Menschen-Pyramiden*), blocked out obelisks
of humanity (*Menschen-Obelisken*): he took a
poor shepherd tribe and fashioned it into a
great people which should also brave centuries,
—a great, eternal, holy people, a people of God,
which could serve all other nations as a
model, nay, as a prototype for the whole of
humanity. He created Israel. As I have
not always spoken with due reverence of
this master, so have I slighted his work.
Yes, to the Jews, to whom the world owes
its God, it also owes His Word, the Bible.
They have saved it out of the bankruptcy of
the Roman empire, and in the wild ruffianism
of the mediæval migration of the peoples
they preserved the dear book, until Protes-
tantism sought for it among them and translated the discovered book into the modern
languages, and distributed it over all the
world.'

Heine has here justly valued the eternal influence which the Jewish teachings and traditions in the Bible have had and will have in all times and climes. He with all historians and moralists has recognised the force of Hebraism in whatever garb, in whatever sect it makes itself felt, as one of the religious currents in civilised morality. And it is ever to be wondered at how the Church, which in every respect arose out of ancient Judaism ; how the Protestant sects, which owe their first light to it and to the Talmud ; how the Puritans, who drew from it not only their religious but even their political inspiration, should have any feeling but that of the kindliest reverence and piety for the people whose whole existence as a nation is based upon the preservation of these immortal documents. The Jews have been and still are the Old Testament transfused into flesh and blood, capable of life and of death and of suffering that lies between the two. And whoever has hurt them by word or deed as Jews, has besmirched and torn the leaves of this great document, adding to it the crime of cruelty in wounding the soul or body of a fellow-man. And woe to him who has the face to do this while he claims for his justification the spirit of love and charity which inspires the writings of the New Testament :

But besides this mission of the Hebrews, which may lie in them as the original bearers of Hebraism, they may have a more direct mission as a people in themselves. Hebraism, in the current sense, has filtered into modern life through numerous channels that may have diverged, or flown in separate courses, far away from the main current of Jewish life. But this main current remains. And here the poetic inspirations of Yehuda-Ben-Halevi may even point to a sober and practical mission which the Jews have hitherto fulfilled, and which may remain for them in the future. Their one great lesson as a people is taught in their continuous martyrdom through so many centuries, the other may have the essence of its effectiveness in the very fact of their dispersion, which even the unbeliever may look upon as a wonderful, if not miraculous, dispensation of Providence.

Their martyrdom is the most colossal instance of the steadfastness in a belief, in a great spiritual idea, to which all elements of life and all instincts for pleasure and even of

self-preservation are sacrificed. To degrade
this steadfastness by calling it obstinacy is
as disingenuous as it is ungenerous. Even if
the object of this great spiritual idea is considered by many as untrue and unworthy of
such sacrifice, the fact of the sacrifice must
remain undisputed ; and wherever moral efforts
are in themselves considered worthy of admiration and respect, there admiration and respect
can never be denied to the Jews. On the
plains of human suffering, throughout the
whole of human history, theirs will be the
highest pyramid of suffering, a great monument
of idealism, the battling with the material to
realise an idea.

Yet in order to make the mission of teaching their spiritual lesson to the world at large
really effective, their dispersion becomes itself a
necessity. And we thus come upon a curious
contradiction in this history of a people : their
insulation on the one hand, and their dispersion on the other. Their insulation was
necessary in order that the teachings of the
moral principles which they embodied should
remain undefiled and uncontaminated throughout the surging waves of history during the
last two thousand years ; their dispersion all

over the world, on the other hand, makes it physically possible that the means of communicating their message are at hand; and when they meet with willing ears into which to pour what good they have to impart, the moral need for this isolation no longer remains. It is then that the phœnix in glowing colours will be called upon to make the last and greatest effort of self-sacrifice to a noble idea: to bury himself and see himself born anew in a more beautiful and resplendent form.

Now to turn to the actual present and the state of affairs we have before us. The Jews are dispersed all over the civilised world, and they have become living portions of the countries in which they live. They are still recognised as Jews, but it is only the form which still separates them from their fellow-citizens. Morally and intellectually there is no appreciable difference between them. Before they thus surrender their own separate existence, it will be right for them to ask whether there is any destiny which at this moment it still remains for them to bear in mind, and, seeing it, conscientiously to live up to. We shall then have to attempt at recognising what practical part the Jews have within the past fifty years played in modern civilisation, and what results of their past history as a race it will be best for them in modern times to attempt at perpetuating and infusing into the general life in which they ought to dissolve. Now, in their practical life also, I look upon the Jews as the chief bearers of what I should like to call spirituality.

It was this spirituality which caused their opposition to the Greeks and to Hellenism with the heathen sensuousness or sensuality. This to a certain degree caused their opposition to the Church of Rome, and made their teachings and principles the arms used by the Puritans against the sensuous side of the Christian Church; and it is this which may lie at bottom of a certain antagonism which exists between the pronounced types of the Jew in Europe and the pronounced representatives of the Northern peoples, especially of the Saxon race.

As stated in the preceding chapter, I do not believe in generalisation based upon ethnological distinctions, and I deny that there is any fixed unity of race among the inhabitants of the north-west of Europe, such as the Germans and the English, or among the Jews on the other hand, which is important in considering any question or measure of practical politics. Still, we may recognise theoretically, if we venture upon a bold generalisation, the ideal type of the pure Saxon race and the pure Jewish race in modern life. And in these exaggerated types we may, it is true, discover an almost essential antagonism. The Jew then stands as the representative of intellectual and emotional sensibility. The direct opposite to this form of Hebraism is not Hellenism, but the pure Germanism which represents the more physical aspect of the soul—namely, character. The Hebrew and the Saxon, in this broadest form of rough generalisation, would thus represent, the one the intellectual and emotional side of man, and the other the substratum to the working of this intellect and emotion, that which remains as a solid basis, the character. To be perfect, each organism must possess the proper balance of both these elements, and the abnormal and diseased forms of life are caused by the undue growth of the one at the cost of the other. The spiritual and intellectual element without the substratum of solidifying character degenerates into subtlety and trickiness, and even cowardice. Character without the infusion of intellectual and emotional sensibility produces stubbornness and brutality. Either of these diseases leads to the caricature of the Jew and of the Teuton. But, fortunately, normal life, with its variety and the interpenetration of different influences, has rectified the possibility of such one-sided developments. The modern Jew who has lived in unhampered intercourse with the Saxon has had this more physical side of his nature developed, and has had moral sturdiness infused; in its spiritual refinement his nature has received more body and substance from it. Similarly the Saxon, notably the German, has derived great benefit from the infusion of that subtler, more active, more refined, and more sensitive element which the Jew has brought into the German communities. It is not a mere matter of chance that with Lessing begins the real German period of enlightenment and of literary taste; that he and Moses Mendelssohn complemented and supplemented one another. I venture to say that it was the infusion of this element, inherent in the Jew, into the German mind and character which to a great extent accounts for the fairest fruits of German culture which the world has reaped within the last hundred years; as the German element, when it did not repress and crush, was needed by the Jew in order to produce such noble, clever, delicately and still strongly organised flowers of humanity as now grace all the intellectual walks of German life in literature, science, and art.

It is, however, true that in cases of social disease, when the social machinery is not properly regulated in itself, and the contending forces are not kept within proper bounds, the one may feast upon the other; they may grow at each other's expense. It is the nature of modern civilised life to favour moral and intellectual forces in their struggle with the physical elements that may contend with them. But this is a matter of historical and social evolution, the result of general causes, with which the Jews have nothing to do. Whether it be deplored or not, it lies so deeply at the foundation of civilised life that we must alter the whole nature of this life if we wish to change any of its manifestations. Yet in so far the Jews need not feel too much offended if they are called parasitic in their function, for it is hardly supposed to mark a lower stage

when the mind feasts upon the body. Yet I
maintain that wherever the Jewish ingenuity
has undermined the economic welfare of the
peasantry or other classes of modern communities, it was either a passing state for
which they cannot be held to account, inasmuch as they were forced to depend exclusively
upon those faculties, being shut out from all
other occupations; or it is simply the outcome of general currents of modern economic
life, for which the Jews are in no way to
be held accountable. Yet the fact remains
that in this capacity, as an intellectual and
emotional force in contradistinction to more
physical forces, the so-called Jew is opposed
to the so-called German, and has always been.

But such *Germanenthum* and such Judaism
are not accurate terms now. The type of the
coarse German is the natural enemy of the
more refined German, as he is of the refined
Jew; and the shifting, tricky, characterless
Jew is as much the enemy of the Jewish man
of honour as he is of the honourable German.
Still, recognising the dangers to which the
exaggerations of his spiritual virtues may lead
him, the Jew must learn his lesson, and try to
guard against any possible disease within his

soul's forces, by emphasising in his education the physical side of his soul, which he can best do by means of a proper culture of his own physique, and of all the habits which such culture leads to. Still, let him cling to the good that has come from the predominance of the spiritual over the sensuous elements in his life and teaching, especially in the opposition to the sensual vices, which (in spite of any individual instance which may be adduced to the contrary) he has kept up in all periods of his history. Let him hand on the torch of purity and temperance which have been one of the chief causes of his wonderful survival during all this period of adversity and of his great success in the walks of life, as well as the ultimate cause of much of the hatred and envy which are showered upon him. This spirituality, strengthened by a continuous persecution from without, has also caused him to turn his affections in an intensified form towards the inner life of his family ; and this piety and devotion of the members of a family to one another, which has clung to the Jew to whatever depths of degradation circumstances may have dragged him, is one of the features which, with the dissolution of his

formal exclusiveness, he must ever keep alive,
hand down, and be the means of diffusing
among the community into which his racial
life will dissolve itself.

This is the mission of the Jews, in so far as
each Jew can act individually upon his surroundings. But there is a mission which, to
use a paradoxical phrase, the Jews have, collectively, as a dispersed race. It is the vocation
of the Jews to facilitate international humanitarianism; and this they will do, and are
doing, not by any doctrinaire effort of individual theorists or preachers, but by their
position of a dispersed people, which has, and
is bound to have, influence.

The present foreign policy of European
states shows a disastrous confusion which
marks a transition. It is the death-struggle of
nationalism, and the transition to a more
active and real form of general international
federation. On the one hand we have the swan-
song of monarchy; dynastic traditions which
belong to the past give form, and often heat
and intensity to a contest which is maintained
by certain customs of diplomatic machinery;
on the other hand is the birth-struggle of the
organisation of international life, the needs of

which are at present only felt practically in the sphere of commerce. This birth-struggle at present manifests itself chiefly in narrow and undignified jealousy and envy for commercial advantages ; and this, unfortunately, is becoming the supreme ultimate aim of all international emulation. We can trace nearly all the diplomatic rivalry ultimately to the interests of commerce and the greed for money. One often hears it said that Jewish bankers make and unmake wars. This is not true. Money makes and unmakes wars ; and if there were not this greed of money among the contending people the bankers would not be called upon at all. There are, of course, further complications favouring the older spirit of national envy, which is dying, though far from being dead. Such are the influences of the huge military organisations, definite wounds unhealed (such as the desire of reprisal on the part of France), and, finally, the last phases of the artificial bolstering-up of the idea of the *national-staat* in Germany and Italy. But the whole of this conception of nationalism, in so far as it implies an initial hatred and enmity towards other national bodies, is doomed. A few generations, perhaps, of disaster and misery accompanying this death-struggle will see the birth of the new era.

Now, there are several practical factors which are paving the way indirectly towards the broader national life of this coming era. They are, strange to say, the two main opposite forces of the economical life of the day—Capital and Labour. Each of these, separately following the inherent impulse of its great forces, which constantly run counter to one another, tends towards the same goal, especially in its pronounced forms. Capital does this in the great international houses and in the Stock Exchanges; Labour, since the first International Convention of 1867, in its great organisations. The highly-developed system of modern banking business and of the Stock Exchange, favoured by the rapid and easy means of intercommunication without regard to distance, has made all countries, however far apart, sensitive to the fate which befalls each; and this tends more and more to make Capital an international unit, which can be, and is being, used, whatever its origin, in all the different quarters where there seems a promising demand for it.[1]

[1] But let no man from the camp of the capitalist (as some anti-Semitic German politicians have endeavoured to do) charge

On the other hand, the growth of organisation among the representatives of labour is fast stepping beyond the narrow limits of national boundaries, and the common interests tend to increase the directness of this wider institution. I am not adducing these facts in order to suggest any solution of the numerous problems which they involve, nor to direct the attention to the interesting historical, economic, and political questions to which they may give rise, but simply to draw attention to the one fact—that in this aspect both capital and labour are effectively paving the way, perhaps unknown to the extreme representatives of either interest, towards the increase of a strong and active cosmopolitan spirit of humanitarianism. And this spirit, at least as an ideal, is certainly dominant in the minds of the best and wisest people of our generation.

Now there will have to be men who, in their nature, as it were their predestination, correspond to this ultimate aim of humanity,

the Jews with being the instigators of Socialism, nor let a Socialist urge his fellow-partisans to an anti-Jewish riot; for the leading spirits of both these antagonistic forces were Jews: the bankers, such as the Rothschilds; and the economists, such as Lasalle and Karl Marx. The capitalists cannot curse the Jews, and the Socialists cannot dynamite the Jews without disowning their very leaders.

and are adapted to this international cosmopolitanism ; and by their sad history and their
international relationship the Jews will be the
fittest bearers of this destiny. Whether near
at hand or remote, this may be the great Messianic era to which we may all look. As far
as outer conditions are concerned, the Jews
are nearest to realising the future ideal of man :
the greatest scope of individual freedom with
the most intense social feeling and organisation.

There is no doubt that this ideal of cosmopolitanism may be a dangerous one, and that
much can be said in favour of the preservation
of our national feeling as a source of inspiration and a motive to ennobling action. George
Eliot, in her *Impressions of Theophrastus Such*,
has argued the case with her usual depth and
clearness. 'That the preservation of national
memories,' she says, ' is an element and a means
of national greatness ; that their revival is a
sign of reviving nationality; that every heroic
defender, every patriotic restorer, has been
inspired by such memories, and has made
them his watchword ; that even such a cor-
porate existence as that of a Roman legion or
an English regiment has been made valorous
by memorial standards—these are the glorious

commonplaces of historic teaching at our public
schools and universities, being happily engrained in Greek and Latin classics.' She then
quotes, as instances of the powerful effect of
such national memories, the restoration of the
modern kingdom of Greece and the establishment of Italy, and repeats Freeman's injunction upon Englishmen to strengthen the
patriotic fibre in them by the infusion of the
great memories of their early Saxon forefathers. 'To this view of our nationality,'
she continues, 'most persons who have feeling and understanding enough to be conscious
of the connection between the patriotic affection and every other affection which lifts us
above emigrating rats and free-loving baboons,
will be disposed to say Amen. . . . The historian
guides us rightly in urging us to dwell on the
virtues of our ancestors with emulation, and
to cherish our sense of a common descent as a
bond of obligation. The eminence, the nobleness of a people depends on its capability of
being stirred by memories, and of striving for
what we call spiritual ends—ends which con-
sist not in immediate material possession, but
in the satisfaction of a great feeling that ani-
mates the collective body as with one soul. A

people having the seed of worthiness in it must feel an answering thrill when it is adjured by the deaths of its heroes who died to preserve its national existence; when it is reminded of its small beginnings and gradual growth through past labours and struggles, such as are still demanded of it in order that the freedom and well-being thus inherited may be transmitted unimpaired to children and children's children; when an appeal against the permission of injustice is made to great precedents in its history and to the better genius breathing in its institutions. It is this living force of sentiment in common which makes a national consciousness. Nations so moved will resist conquest with the very breasts of their women, will pay their millions and their blood to abolish slavery, will share privation in famine and all calamity, will produce poets to sing "some great story of a man," and thinkers whose theories will bear the test of action. An individual man, to be harmoniously great, must belong to a nation of this order, if not in actual existence, yet existing in the past, in memory, as a departed, invisible, beloved ideal, once a reality, and perhaps to be restored. A common humanity is not yet enough to feed the rich blood of various activity which makes a complete man. The time is not come for cosmopolitanism to be highly virtuous, any more than for communism to suffice for social energy. . . . For, to repeat, not only the nobleness of a nation depends on the presence of this national consciousness, but also the nobleness of each individual citizen. Our dignity and rectitude are proportioned to our sense of relationship with something great, admirable, pregnant with high possibilities, worthy of sacrifice, a continual inspiration to self-repression and discipline by the presentation of aims larger and more attractive to our generous part than the securing of personal ease or prosperity.

'And a people possessing this good should surely feel not only a ready sympathy with the effort of those who, having lost the good, strive to regain it, but a profound pity for any degradation resulting from its loss; nay, something more than pity when happier nationalities have made victims of the unfortunate whose memories nevertheless are the very fountain to which the persecutors trace their most vaunted blessings.' She then continues, while powerfully refuting the prejudices against the Jews, to argue in favour of the retention and even restoration of their nationality.

Though I am heartily in sympathy with the whole of this remarkable essay of hers, I do not agree with her in considering it desirable that the Jewish nationality should be restored, at least as far as the Occidental Jews are concerned. Nor do I think it desirable that they should dwell to any practical extent upon the memories of the past history of the Jews, even though they may cling to Judaism, by which I mean the Jewish religion, with all its traditions of the past. For Judaism does not interfere with the feeling of national patriotism for the Western country in which the Jew is born and his ancestors have lived, any more than Christianity does with its own traditions of the past. The English, the Germans, the Dutch, the French and the Italians are most of them Christians, and many may be imbued with the great traditions of their Church; but this will make them none the less English, Germans, Dutchmen, Frenchmen, or Italians. This only applies to religion, and not to race. The inspiring influences of the past which George Eliot so eloquently puts forward, need not be confounded as regards the Occidental Jew with the racial history of the Jews. The English, the German, or the French Jew has to the same degree the heritage of the great past of England, Germany, and France as any other citizen of these nations; and if he have not immediate Saxon, Teutonic, or Burgundian descent, neither have those of Norman or Celtic, of Wendish or Slav, of Breton or pure Gallic blood. The inspiring influences of the past need not be less potent for being clearly defined within the period of more accurate history, and for being despoiled of the nebulous tradition of uncertain ethnological hypotheses.

I am also in sympathy with George Eliot when she says that the time is not come for cosmopolitanism to be highly virtuous, but I do look upon a certain form of cosmopolitanism as a practical ideal which it is well for us to hold before us. And I venture to believe that this great novelist and philosopher would have agreed with me. I know that many thoughtful people are repelled by the idea of cosmopolitanism because of their love of 'individuality.' They consider the free and varied expression of the inner and outer capabilities of single men and of larger bodies of men to be one of the most desirable conditions of life. With this

I also agree. But I do not consider cosmopolitanism, as I conceive it, as in any way destructive of individuality; on the contrary, I think it will further it. The analogy, which I do not wish to pursue further, at once suggests itself between cosmopolitanism and restricted nationalism on the one hand, and free-trade and protection in economic life on the other. Cosmopolitanism will, I trust, encourage rather than repress the desirable expression of individuality both for states and for individuals. Federation of states (by which I emphatically do not mean centralisation of life, interest, and of intellectual leadership within one metropolis) gives perhaps a greater chance for the free expression of individual characteristics within the proper channels of activity. The natural conditions, the local differences, will of themselves work in this direction; and we can see how they are acting in the United States of America, where, I should say, there is in many respects a growth rather than a decrease of individualisation in the various districts. It is true we do notice the dying away of local peculiarities, costume, habits of living and of uncleanliness in the remoter districts of Europe; but this is not due to the action of the cosmopolitan spirit, but to rapid communication, the spread of education, and other influences. And in estimating these changes we must carefully guard against attaching too much weight to our own selfish artistic interest and craving for the picturesque, in which, under the veil of philanthropy, we may be looking upon our fellow-men as puppets that are dancing for our edification upon a miniature stage of our own making. Frenchmen, Englishmen, Italians, Germans, and Americans are pronounced in their individuality, and will remain so for ages to come, in spite of the growth of the cosmopolitan spirit; and we need not be much afraid of its extinction. But what cosmopolitanism must set itself to counteract is not the positive expression of individuality, but its negative attitude. We hope that national traditions will remain in their inspiring force, but that national antagonisms and jealousies will grow less intense and perhaps cease; that, as they go, more active steps for friendly intercommunication will be made; that commercial and industrial life will be ordered and regulated and elevated out of the chaotic state of futile internecine waste and destruction. We hope that civilised peoples

will really live up to the feelings, which in all
other respects they have, of the common ties of
civilisation, and in so far of a common history.
This will be the basis of the feeling for cosmopolitanism which we hold as a practical ideal,
and from being a feeling it will lead to definite
and direct beneficent action.

The essence of cosmopolitanism is the
widening of human sympathies; and it is as
false to think that it will lead to the weaken-
ing of proper national feeling, as it is an
error to believe that the widening of our
sympathies makes them less intense, and
weakens our power of affection. It is said
that charity begins at home ; it might with
equal truth be maintained that charity begins
away from home; that in a measure, as it is
really removed from self, does it become charity
in the truest sense. The physical analogy
which people unconsciously have in their
minds when they misunderstand the nature
of sympathy, is drawn from the world of solid
or fluid bodies. The more you extend these,
the wider you spread them, the less will they
have in depth. And so it is supposed that the
wider the area over which you extend your
sympathies, the less will be their depth at any

given point. But this analogy is misleading. Sympathy is life, and not matter; it is a high function of a highly organised body; the more you exercise this function, the more you increase your heart's vitality in different directions, the greater will be the force when concentrated into one effort. The narrowing and cramping of sympathies leads to atrophy of the affections; give them play, and they will retain their health and vitality. I would appeal to the actual observation and experience of the reader with regard to the life that he knows intimately and can see about him. Will he not find that people whose sympathies and affections are bounded by their own families, with a negative attitude towards people beyond these bounds, are not as considerate and sympathetic to the members of their own family as those whose sympathies know no such narrow restrictions? For love, unless guided by sympathy, is closely akin to selfishness. And the further you proceed in the scale, the more you will realise this. Wherever there is a marked negative boundary to the affections, be it by the clan, or the township, or the county, or the country, these affections are not proof against trials, they are not so thor-

oughly permeated by right altruistic thought
as where unselfishness has been raised into a
positive faculty by being removed habitually
away from the centre of self. The man who
only loves himself does not love himself well.
He has not practised putting himself into other
people's places, and he will therefore be unjust
to himself, and dissatisfied when his immediate
desires are thwarted.

On this account I maintain that cosmopolitanism, which means an effective widening of
national sympathies, will in no way diminish
our power of national affection.

Yet, in spite of this ultimate ideal of the
future of humanity, the question will come to
the Jew, as well as to others, what is the
immediate duty of each citizen in a civilised
state who holds such an ideal? And here
again the Jew, in his own history and in the
contradictory elements which his fate has
united in him, approaches nearest to a possible
solution. He has, on the one hand, the intense
love of family, and, on the other, the history
of his people presents to him the feeling of a
dispersion over the earth. Joining the spirit
of these two facts together, he can thus solve
the problem which vexes many a thoughtful

and conscientious citizen in our days: the
difficulty of bringing into harmony the dictates
of patriotism and the love of humanity. Just
as in him the tangible and actively moving
impulse of affection for those that are immediately about him in no way kept him from
being stirred by the intangible ties which
bound him to his distant co-religionists, of
whose physical existence he had no perceptible
evidence, so he can realise how the duties
of patriotism can fill his soul, and still leave
room for active sympathy with his fellow-men
in other countries. We have, on the one hand,
the ultimate idea of cosmopolitanism, on the
other, the immediate love, loyalty, and self-
sacrificing energy of the home-feeling in
patriotism. Now, the fusing force which
binds these two ideal factors together, which
makes cosmopolitanism more and more a
necessity, and which at the same time can
direct the course of patriotism, is the Hellenic
idea of culture and civilisation. In making
each home and each state the most civilised
and cultured possible, we necessarily, *de
facto*, approach cosmopolitanism. This idea
(whether the practical politician is conscious of
it or not) is at present the highest touchstone

—the ideal foundation of all our national and international policy. Whatever adds to the growth of this civilisation is good for the separate state, and at the same time tends to the ultimate ideal of cosmopolitanism, which ideal is not furthered by the denial of national ties and the coquetting with premature figments of unsound cosmopolitanism. And, on the other hand, whatever tends to oppose this growth of civilisation, in all its forms, is bad for the separate state, for national and international life. It is thus that Hebraism and Hellenism—contending with one another in Philo, declared by Heine to be divorced—will ultimately be fused together in a modern life.

There is a curious analogy, within a marked difference, between the modern Greek nation and the Jews. As in their dispersion the Jews are the most tangible and purest representatives of Hebraism, however weak and however dispersed, so the modern Greek state is the most tangible remnant of ancient Hellenism. But as Hebraism consists in purely intellectual and moral ideas, whereas Hellenism appeals to the more sensuous and æsthetic faculties, the physically perceptible representation of Hellenism is necessarily associated with the works, remains, literature, and local associations of the country. Therefore it is to be found in the Greek land and in the country's monuments. The Greeks, therefore, fulfil their ideal vocation in concentration in their own country itself, and in regenerating and revivifying our classical associations : whereas the Jews fulfil their vocation in their very dispersion. But if the modern Greeks and the modern Jews are conscious of this their highest vocation, they must have the motto, *noblesse oblige*. They have a great past history to live up to, and their duties will be greater than those of their other fellow-citizens.

And for those who are not Jews, realising the great past history of this people, feeling what in their dispersion and suffering they stand for, as the living bearers of high ideals, it will be their duty to favour and not to repress their fellow-citizens who spring from this oldest of peoples. I would appeal to the sense of chivalry which rules the social actions of every gentleman, that he should respect the dignity of these people. The Decalogue was the foundation of our social morality ; but as our life has developed, so have the spheres of possible wrong-doing been multiplied and diversified. These laws will always remain, and have for the greater part been incorporated into our civic law. We are not likely to steal and murder, but we are likely to kill the dignity and self-respect of our neighbours. And if not as gentlemen and as men of noble and generous hearts, then as Christians, we are bound to respect and to succour those who may not be placed in the same advantageous position as we are. Where is the love preached by Christ, if we wound the sensibilities of our neighbour and draw the heart-blood of his self-esteem ?

And as for the Jew, if he dwell upon the past history of his ancestors, he may feel the modest pride, the joy of knowing that he belongs to the oldest of civilised races, which has continually handed on the torch of truth and enlightenment for centuries, during which the peoples of Europe were even wallowing in brutality and ignorance. Holding the high ideal mission which his descent has laid upon him before his eyes, let him devote his energies to the national life in which he is born. He will then be able to ignore the petty slurs that may be cast upon him by ignorance, and, maintaining his dignified modesty, let him feel that whosoever flaunts his apparent social advantages into his face is a snob, whether he be a prince of the blood or a leader of modern politics.

III

THE SOCIAL POSITION OF THE JEWS IN THE MIDDLE AGES AND MODERN TIMES.

THE late Mr. James Russell Lowell was wont to say that a large proportion of the great families of the English aristocracy had some admixture of Jewish blood, while some of the great names were in a direct line to be traced back to Jewish ancestors.[1] Of course such conversational statements must not be taken literally. Many years ago I met a Russian scholar, deeply read in literature and science—the pure Russian without any

[1] For the Middle Ages we may here quote the patrician family of the Pierleone, which emanated from the Roman Ghetto, counted among its members a pope, a queen (from whom many European monarchs are descended), and even in the fifteenth century maintained that the house of Hapsburg (Comites Montes Aventini) was founded by two brothers Pierleone who settled in Austria. In more modern times the house of Saxe-Coburg-Kohary, members of which are seated on two thrones (Portugal and Bulgaria) are on the mother's side descended from the daughter of a Jewish-Hungarian nobleman named Kohary.

associations with Jews—who told me that he was engaged upon a work which set itself the task of tracing the origin of most of the great men in science and letters that were then living in Germany; and that he was coming to the conclusion that, not only were a great many of them actually Jews, but that a large proportion of the best known among the Christian dignitaries had also some admixture of Jewish blood.

If we look about us in modern history from the Middle Ages onwards, and realise the vast number of Jews, or those whose parents had been Jews, who were to be found in exalted positions—popes and archbishops, kings and queens, statesmen and ambassadors, great financiers, men of science and letters, artists and scholars—our first astonishment at such statements as those I have just quoted will be considerably diminished. Our estimate of the social position and qualifications of the Jews will become essentially modified. We shall perhaps even be able to sympathise with the racial self-confidence of Disraeli as flaunted before the snub-nosed Saxon. At all events, we shall not be able any longer to maintain the ignorant position with regard to the social qualifications of these people held by those who only know of either the Biblical Jew or the Old-clothes Jew, who may, when hard pressed, grant to these people the possession of certain moral qualities, but never dream of taking them into consideration in questions of claims to social distinction.

Yet I venture to maintain, that if within the next century feelings of social consideration based upon ancestry still exist, whosoever can then point to pure Jewish ancestry will find a source whence flow social advantages as great as now fall to those who can trace their lineage back to the Crusaders; for they will then be immediately connected with a group of people whose high merits in the present and great distinction in the past will be universally admitted.

To support this bold and perhaps startling proposition we must first examine into the nature of the causes which in general lead to social distinction, and then see how they apply to the Jews.

In stating causes which underlie social evolution we cannot hope to be exhaustive, and must before all limit our scope. Some must be excluded because they are too restricted in their influence; others because they are too wide in the ramification of the subject. So, for instance, I should exclude organised and stereotyped aristocracies where certain functions in the state—for instance, a seat in the House of Lords—give a fixed and tangible centre of social influence. Yet in England the peerage has ever been fluctuating; it has thus remained in touch with the other spheres of social life, and is in so far subject to the natural causes which govern this general life in its social evolution. I should also exclude from this inquiry the earliest prehistoric periods in the history of human society, when mythical connection was sought for in the ancestry of those who claimed social distinction. Such inquiry would lead us too far into a field at present rife with numerous, even divergent, hypotheses. It is best to turn our eyes first upon the simpler communities whose life we have before us within reach, and then upon the more complex life of larger communities, where, however, these causes become readily manifest in their comparatively simple activity. We find then that one of the simplest and most universal causes for social distinction lies in the fact of being universally known or known to a great many. And this simple cause has been most persistently active in this direction from the earliest time to our own day, in the most remote savage community as in the modern city of London. Negatively, we find him despised who is not known, who is 'a nobody, a foreigner.' The terms noble (*nobilis*), ignoble (*ignobilis*), are immediately derived from the Latin verb 'to know,' and point to this fact of being known or unknown. This fact, in connection with others (domestic complications and unfavourable conditions of education), has had much to do with the disadvantages under which the bastard laboured. He was a man in whose existence important facts were not known. The more complete this knowledge concerning the life of each individual, the further back in his own history and antecedents one could go, the greater were the possibilities with regard to social recognition. And out of this sprang the idea associated with the phrase 'pure blood' or 'thoroughbred,' which developed into the idea of the ruling classes. In more complex developments this continuity is not taken literally. It often suffices to point to such favourable conditions in the past, though they may have been interrupted. This, for instance, would be the .case with the French *émigrés* after the Revolution, or the Huguenots, etc.

Besides this factor of pure blood in simpler communities, one cause for social distinction appears to be length of settlement in the country. This is especially noticeable in the younger and colonial settlements that are now growing up, though it is not unknown in many of the oldest communities, especially when they are on a small scale. There are many deeper reasons for this. There is, for instance, a certain prescribed right to the soil and connection with it to be derived from the length of settlement upon it, and every new-comer is in so far an intruder. Then, again, length of settlement is conducive to the complete knowledge of the people thus settled, which we have just seen is one of these social qualifications. And, finally, in a more complex form, the earliest settlers readily develop into a compact set, into which each new-comer must singly work his way, and the older compact body will thus be conscious of and assert its power.

This claim of length of settlement becomes still stronger when coupled with wealth and ease, which, while freeing the individual from occupations which are considered debasing or unfavourable to social education, give him the opportunity of choosing vocations which in themselves command recognition and consideration. Here we are in danger of being tempted into deeper moral and intellectual analysis than this study of the surface-life of communities demands. Suffice it to say, that wealth and ease, together with length of settlement, are most likely in themselves to confer social distinction, independently of the individual character and attainment of exceptional men who do not depend upon general influences.

When society becomes more developed in larger communities—in towns, and in the metropolis, with complex organisation—there is a tendency to specialise the various departments of life, and to dissociate them from one another, so that we then have a definitely organised 'social' life. There are set at work the factors which lead to a social selection, which may be a form of natural selection or of very unnatural selection. The social birds of a feather will then flock together and will form sets. But within these different sets, again, there will be some who more or less directly and specially flock together because of social qualities which will be recognised by most, if not all sets. These conditions will be outer qualities or inner qualities. The outer qualities will again be found in wealth, which gives the power of entertaining and leisure for developing and utilising this power, or occupations which many have in common, and which exclude the rivalry and competition which is self-centred and, in so far, unsocial. Leisure occupations, such as sport of all kind, are in themselves social, inasmuch as they depend upon a number of people acting together, and also in that they bring people of such similar tastes together.

The inner conditions are often similar religious beliefs and intellectual pursuits which tend to give this sense of social comradeship. But it will readily be seen that in this more complex organisation and the action of such social selection we have a fluctuating quantity, varying with the duration of such a definite set, and with the estimation in which certain tastes or pursuits are at any time held.

A curious fact in the working of these social forces is the repugnance which is felt for the *parvenu* and the pusher, and the tendency

towards what may be called meritless distinction. We may be fast working out of this,
but it certainly does at present remain active
to a certain degree. There is an opposition to
him who manifestly craves for social admission
and evidently strives for it. The result is that
it is considered desirable that the social distinction should be of earlier date than the life
of the aspirant, not so much on account of the
age, as that it must not be the result of his own
effort. There is at bottom some right instinct
in this apparently immoral condition, inasmuch
as the nature of purely social intercourse is
playful, neither moral nor intellectual, but
artistic. Whenever we are to appeal to the
social instinct through the moral or intellectual channels, we are at once put into the
mood of serious thought and not of social play.
There is also at bottom a right instinct, probably based upon the experience of impersonal
society, in the opposition to those who have
immediately acquired wealth or position by
means of their own effort, inasmuch as they
have often been so much engrossed in the
struggle that it has led to a neglect of the
lighter social faculties. So much is right in
the tendency towards meritless distinction.

But of course there are so many other elements connected with moral and intellectual life which are here left out of sight that the whole will not bear close scrutiny.

What we may select as the broader and lasting elements which have qualified socially, and will do so to a lesser or greater degree in the future, are, first, the element of pure blood; second, the length of settlement; and third, the essential and most important of all, the position in life which raised the member into the spheres which qualify socially—either a position of eminence in the commonwealth, or one which in itself gives the opportunities for refined tastes, or the intellectual and moral superiority which are most likely to lead to all these qualities.

Now I maintain that the Jews, as a people and as individuals, have possessed these to the very highest degree, and it is from this point of view I wish to examine their history.

Leaving aside the persecutions which came periodically over Europe like diseases, the lowering of the social position of the Jews as a body dates from the general emancipation of European peoples in modern times, and especially since the French Revolution. In the

Middle Ages they were a more separate body, with their own autonomy and jurisdiction, and their own social standards, generally based upon high intellectual and moral attainments. In many places where there was no pronounced class of burghers, they supplied this class—separated on the one hand from the nobles, on the other from the serfs. They were certainly nearer to, and better understood and valued by, the nobles than by the serfs. Not being either nobles or of the clerical or serf class, there was no standard by which to judge them socially; they were simply themselves, and maintained their inner superiority, together with the consideration of the superior classes, with whom they were not infrequently allied by marriage and conversion.

All through the Middle Ages and the Renaissance their general social position was either very high, or it was distinctly itself. They were not to be classed definitely by comparison with the outer world, but were dependent upon their own outer and inner standards.

When this separateness was broken up, and the lower orders were more and more emancipated, the Jews lost this inner standard of their own, while the former serfs or poor burghers looked upon them as their equals, and attempted in every way to make them their social inferiors.

Being in the majority, these lower orders, of course, often carried the point in the eyes of the world; and the Jews themselves, losing the intellectual vigour of their own inner organisation, began to degenerate; though they have, even as a body, ever maintained a moral and intellectual superiority as compared with the classes among whom they would roughly be grouped now.

As to purity of blood, in whatever sense this may be taken, there is no European race or section of one that can vie with them.

I have urged above that, for any practical purpose, for purposes of practical politics (to cause a pro-Semitic or an anti-Semitic movement), we cannot now speak of unity of race, especially when we consider the many centuries during which different portions of the race have dwelt continuously in various countries, if not in different sections of the globe. We must also consider the vicissitudes of life in the many unsettled periods through which any race must have passed during the barbarous ages. Even in the third century a charac-

teristic answer was given to the famous Rabbi
Juda, called forth by his racial pride. Juda
Bar Jecheskel, chief of the Babylonian community, was born A.D. 225, and died A.D. 299.
Juda was so particular of the purity of Jewish
blood that he kept his son Isaac unmarried
long beyond the customary age, because he
was not satisfied with the pedigrees of the
families from which he was to choose a wife
for him. Ulla, one of those learned in the law,
remarked to him: 'Can we be quite certain
that we are not descended from some of the
Pagans who, at the destruction of Jerusalem,
ravished the maidens in Zion?'[1]

With these restrictions in the light of the
less important social considerations, the fact
remains that they are the purest race. Whether
Weissman is right or not in his limitations
to the generally current views of evolution
and heredity, whether acquired habits and

---

[1] In mitigation of Juda's pride another story concerning
him, told by Graetz, must be remembered as showing his
strong sense of justice, which in a wholesome manner counteracted and purified the aristocratic nature of these communities. He laid a ban upon a distinguished member of the
college of rabbis because of his doubtful morality. When
he visited him on his death-bed, he said frankly to him, 'I
am proud that no impulse of partiality led me to spare even a
man of your blood and position.'

those outer conditions pressing upon individual
life affect the organism so that it immediately
transmits these adaptations to its progeny or
not, the fact remains that the physical and
moral qualities which have caused this race
to survive must point to a process of natural
selection which, in the animal world, we
should certainly characterise by the term
'thoroughbred.'   And however these wider
theories of natural laws affect social life, I
firmly hold that such enduring broad qualities
of a race will, other things being equal, lead
its individual members to the foreground
under any conditions of life, be they physical,
moral, intellectual, or social.   At all events,
the fact remains that, from the superficial
social point of view, so far as 'purity of
blood' may be claimed as one of the conditions of social distinction, the Jews have this
claim above all other people of European descent.   But it may be urged that the idea of
'purity of blood' implies the inheritance of
those conditions of living which produce refined life with refined tastes.   Grave doubts
may then be entertained whether such conditions are actually transmitted by individual
inheritance; or whether it is not merely the

transmission of a general tradition. But I shall show that those conditions of refined life have existed for a longer time, and more continuously, with the Jews than with any other people.

Now as to antiquity of settlement. If we consider the constant changes in the ethnological geography of Europe after the downfall of classical Rome (nay, even prior to it), the nomadic character of the migration of the races sweeping from east to west, from north to south, we may certainly count the Jews as among the oldest inhabitants of Europe.

To leave aside the question of classical and biblical periods (where much can be said for them as colonists in Europe), they certainly were numerously settled in Italy even in the times of the Republic and during the Roman empire, and have been there continuously down to our day, in spite of the numerous persecutions and expulsions. After the disruption of the Roman empire there certainly was a Jewish community at Ravenna in the sixth century. In the south there were large numbers at Naples, at Venusium (the birthplace of Horace), at Palermo, Messina, and Agrigentum. Under Theodoric, himself an

Aryan, their position was a favourable one; there were synagogues and communities at Milan, Genoa, and most of the north Italian cities, and at Rome Theodoric defended them against the attacks of the catholic Christians. They proved their loyalty to their Gothic friend by supporting his successor Theodatos, and fighting desperately for him at the siege of Naples, when they were the last to be overcome by Belisarius. Their free position continued under the Lombards, while even Gregory I., in spite of his keen desire to see them converted, did not allow his zeal to take an aggressive form. Since then there have always been Jews in Italy.

They were still more firmly rooted in France and Spain. In the west of Europe the Catholic Church advanced but slowly, and was long before it was able to hurl its power against the Jews. They thus held important positions in these countries from the earliest times down to the advanced Middle Ages.

The first migration of the Jews into these countries falls in the time of the Roman Republic and Cæsar. They were either led there as merchants or sent there as prisoners, but in either case they enjoyed full citizenship. The conquering Franks or Burgundians looked upon them as Romans. The earliest Frankish laws make no special distinction between them. Under Chlovis they lived in Auvergne (Avverna), Carcasonne, Orleans, Paris, and in Belgium. They were so numerous in the ancient Greek port of Massilia (Marseilles) that this city was called 'the Hebrew City'; they were also numerous at Arles, in both of which places they used the Greek language. Near Narbonne a mountain was called *mons Judaicus*. These Frankish or Burgundian Jews were engaged in agriculture, trade, and commerce, and were in intimate intercourse with all classes of their fellow-inhabitants, from the princes to the common people; they often married Christian wives, and stood in friendly relation to the Christian priests, notably to Bishop Hilarius of Arles (who maintained a somewhat independent position towards Rome). At his death they were as distressed as were those of his own Christian flock, and at his funeral they wept and mingled their Hebrew dirges with the litanies of the Church. Jews and Christians met at feasts and meals, so much so that the Council of Vannes (A.D. 465) decreed that it was not law-

ful for priests to take part in Jewish meals,
' for it was not dignified that while the Christians partook of the meals of the Jews, the
Jews spurned the food of the Christians, and
so gave the appearance as if the priests were
lower in standing than the Jews.' Though
under Chlovis this relation remained unaltered,
the Burgundians were more eager in matters
of the Catholic Church, and from the time of
Sigismund (A.D. 516) attempts were made to
forbid this free intercourse.

The Franks were also influenced by the
tendency, though even among them the de-
centralisation of the rule caused it to affect
only single districts, so that secular and clerical
princes still lived in friendly converse with
them. But the centre of ill-feeling against the
Jews emanated from the Bishop of Arverna
(Avitus), who lived at Clermont. In this city
the Jews were persecuted in A.D. 576, and
then fled to Marseilles. From this moment
the movement against them increased, but
slackened again under Pipin and his successors.
We shall have to speak of the higher and
firmer position they acquired under Charlemagne in dealing with their social character :
but it will suffice for us to realise that, despite

the persecution in France, they have been residents there from the earliest times. Especially in the south and at Bordeaux they have been continuous settlers, not unfrequently of great distinction and of high position.

In Germany they have been settled since the remotest antiquity—I venture to say as long as any class or race of people whom we can now identify, and much longer than most. They are in this sense, and from this point of view, much more Germanic than most of the inhabitants of Prussia and the other Slav districts of modern Germany.

An old chronicler considers the Jews settled on the Rhine as being the descendants of the legions which had taken part in the burning of the Temple. He maintains that the Vangioni had chosen beautiful wives out of the numerous Jewish prisoners, and had taken them with them to their homes on the banks of the Rhine and the Main. The children born of Germanic fathers and Jewish mothers were educated by their mothers in the Jewish faith, as the fathers did not look after them. These children of mixed race are supposed to be the founders of the Jewish communities between Mayence and Worms. It is

historically certain that in the Roman colony
of Cologne there was a Jewish community
before Christianity had come to power under
Constantine.   The leaders and distinguished
members of these congregations had conferred
upon them by the pre-Christian emperors the
privilege of exclusion from the burdensome
civic offices.   Constantine rescinded this
privilege, and only reserved it for two or
three families.   The Jews of Cologne also had
the privilege of separate jurisdiction, which
they retained far into the Middle Ages.   A
non-Jewish plaintiff, even a priest, had to bring
his suit against a Jew before the Jewish judge
(Jew-bishop).   Since those days the Jews
have ever been settled in Germany; and
though, during periods of barbarous persecution, they may have been forced to exchange
temporarily one district of the country for
another, the numerous principalities into which
Germany was divided enabled them always
to remain in Germany proper.   These changes
of abode, moreover, did not make their domicile in Germany as a whole any less fixed
than did the wanderings of other constituent
elements of Germany's population—from the
great premediaeval migrations, through the

Thirty Years' War, and the wars of more modern history—make theirs illusory. At all events, we are justified in maintaining that the Jews have become an integral part of the German people as they now exist; that they have contributed more than their share (taken in numerical proportion) to the establishment of what we consider best in German spirit and culture; and that their social rights, on the ground of length of domicile, are beyond all contention.

In Spain the Jews were certainly among the earliest settlers. Their immigration into some districts goes back to the nebulous period of prehistoric times. They certainly were there as freemen during the age of the Roman Republic. And in Paul's time there was an enormous Jewish population—so large that, according to Church historians, their presence there appears to have been the cause of his visit to Hesperia. Strabo tells us that they had become so thoroughly latinised that in some districts they had forgotten their own language and only spoke Latin. The canons of the Synods of Elvira and Toledo refer to the fact that they had come to Spain before the Christians, and possessed greater wealth

and power than them. Their numbers may
be estimated from the fact that Granada formerly was called the 'Jews' City,' because it
was almost entirely inhabited by Jews; so also
Tarragona.   In Cordova there was a gate called
the Jews' Gate, and a fortress at Saragossa
was called by the Arabs Ruta al Jahud.   It
is likely, from the discovery of a sepulchral
slab to a Jewess (whose names were Belliosa
and Miriam), which is written in Hebrew,
Greek, and Latin, that these Jews originally
came from Greek-speaking countries.   Though
under the Goths, and later through the Inquisition, they suffered the most cruel persecution, their social standing, as I shall have
occasion to show, was of the highest until
their expulsion in the fifteenth century.
Among themselves they formed a highly cultured and brilliant society, far above that of
the upper classes of the rest of Europe, and
through intermarriage and by the forcible conversion of many of their members they were
related to the great houses of Spain; so that it
is maintained by some that many of the prominent 'grandees' of Spain are of Jewish blood.

After their expulsion from Spain and
Portugal many of these Jews settled in Hol-

land and England, in both of which countries
there had been Jewish inhabitants long before.
In Holland there had already been a number
of Jews, and after the Spanish Inquisition
many Marranos or Nuevos Cristianos (those
forcibly converted to Christianity, but at heart
Jews) settled there, the movement beginning
with the romantic immigration of Maria Nuñes
and her party. The idea of seeking refuge in
Holland seems to have originated in a brave
woman, a Neo-Christian. She, as well as her
husband, Gaspar Lopes Homem, and their children, were Jews at heart, though they belonged
to the converted families, and they desired to
return to Judaism. When a ship under Jacob
Tirado secretly left Portugal, she sent her son
and her daughter, Maria Nuñes, famous for her
beauty, with him. An English frigate captured the Portuguese vessel. The commander
of this vessel, an English duke, was so much
attracted by Maria Nuñes that he offered her
marriage, which she refused. When the cap-
tives were led to London the beauty of Maria
caused such sensation that Queen Elizabeth
was anxious to make the acquaintance of the
girl who had refused a duke. She invited
her to an audience, and drove through the

streets of London with her.   Probably through her influence these captive Marranos were enabled to leave England and to continue their voyage to Holland.   Men like Tirado himself—Samuel Pollache, Jakob Israel Belmonte (a Jewish poet, author of the epic 'Job '), Alonso de Herrera (descendant of Gonsalos de Cordova, the conqueror of Naples)—were the chief members of these settlements.

In England, as well as in the French possessions of Henry II., and other English kings, large numbers of Jews lived.   They were so wealthy that their houses were like palaces. Many Englishmen were so partial to the Jewish faith that they joined the Jewish communities.   There was one such community existing, composed exclusively of converts to Judaism.   Many of the great families of England from that time and in later ages are thus connected with the Jewish people.   But, beginning with the massacre at the coronation of Richard Cœur de Lion, and culminating in the cruel assassination of the rich Jews of York, Lynn, Norwich, Bury St. Edmunds, the persecutions became such, fanned by the fanaticism of the priests, that they were driven out of England for two hundred and fifty years, and only returned again in the sixteenth century. It was then, owing to the favourable disposition of Cromwell and the Roundheads to the Jews, that the exertions of Manasse Ben Israel found ready response. But it was not until the accession of Charles II. that they resettled in England in larger numbers. Since then they have lived in England undisturbed without any repression to the present day.

The Spanish Inquisition also led large numbers to the West Indies, Brazil, South America in general, and to North America. It is now maintained on good authority that they were directly concerned in the expedition of Columbus. Jews certainly settled in New York as early as 1654, and they were among the first settlers of Newport, Charleston, Savannah, Baltimore, and other cities of the United States, who brought the great inter-oceanic commerce to these places.

To turn now to the refinement of life and thought which are conducive to higher social qualifications, I would compare the Jewish people as a whole, including the lowest classes, with those of other nationalities and character.

It must often have struck an observer of English life how readily a person of Jewish extraction, rising from humble to brilliant conditions of life, adapts himself to the manners and customs of those with whom he lives, and is felt by his associates to be at one with them in tastes and habits. And this peculiarity is the more markedly noticeable when such a person is compared with one who has risen from humbler conditions of what might be called 'dissenting' antecedents some fifty years ago. The chief reason for this is, in my opinion, to be found in the fact that the life of a Jew as such, to whatever class he belonged or in whatever country he lived, or, finally, in whatever period of the history of this people, was never devoid of elements of refinement which are essential to Judaism itself.

Coarse and brutal plebeianism, without the elevation of spiritual refinement, is impossible to those who are truly Jews. It is prevented by many essential features of their national life; among them I would first enumerate their inner family life, fixed by the laws of the Decalogue, fostered by all religious traditions, and intensified by their long martyrdom and the adversity and cruelty they have met with for so many centuries in their outer life. It is this which, together with other elements in

their inner history, has counteracted the hard-
ening and embittering and lowering tendencies
of the dire fate which cruelty and brutal ignorance have for so long forced upon them. The degradation of the soul can never work its down-
ward course where the elevation of religious
faith and its spiritual surroundings are made
physically potent by the daily appeal to the
best feelings of love and self-sacrifice urging
on to definite action in the home. The Germans have two almost untranslatable words:
Gemüthsleben and *Gemüthsbildung*, the life of
the heart and the education of the heart. The
intellectual education of the school and the
training of character in the life of the outer
world cannot readily develop this more emotional side of the soul: the appeal to the
affections and to the faculty of sympathy, the
subjection, control, and refinement of passion
—all these are the corner-stone to the most
artistic structure of the soul's life, which forms
taste. A man or a woman with a wide scale
of affections and with all-penetrating sympathy
must, in some form, be possessed of tact, and
cannot do what is absolutely in bad taste.

The most abject picture of unpoetic occupation and outer life in a Jewish household is

always relieved and redeemed by the soften-
ing light of their family and home existence.
George Eliot has in *Daniel Deronda* described
this fact in a very striking manner in her picture of the family Cohen, with their concentration upon the meanest life of gain, only
relieved and beautified by the mellowness of
their family life.   Without this, the lowering
influence of such occupation would, in all other
cases, lead to the meanest degradation.   Considering that in some countries, and in the
last centuries, the Jews have often been forced
into the occupations most trying to the maintenance of noble character, it must be considered nothing short of a miracle that they
have retained the qualities they possess, if it
were not for these refining and ennobling
counteractants.

Now, this family life and its influence are
not dependent upon the individual nature of
one family, but they were made a Jewish
characteristic by the nature of their religious
life in all times.   In spite of the hieratic con-
stitution of the Jewish polity during its independence, the Jewish religion has, certainly in
later times, never tended towards the organisation of a church as independent from the

family. And this tendency has manifested itself, first, in that the rights and ceremonies and religious functions were not relegated to the clergy in the Church, but were made a part of the family life, uniting the members for this purpose, the father taking the position of the priest; and, secondly, in that religion was not merely formalised and made a matter referring to the supernatural, celestial life and world, but permeated and entered into the immediate daily life, as is shown by the Talmud and the literature which has grown up out of it.

The religious functions and ceremonies thus elevated and ennobled the family life. The miserable second-hand shop, the hovel of the peddler, are transformed into a temple for the time being, of which the pattern is the great temple of Jerusalem: and the warm imagination of this people, developed and nurtured by the hardness and sordidness of the life without, invests it with all the glories of its golden prototype. The peddler, who during the week is bowed down beneath the weight of the sack he carries along the road, the vendor and buyer of old clothes, is the high-priest of this tabernacle and is upraised in the sense of his dignity. On the Friday evening, under the lighted lamps which retain the shape of the golden lamps of Jerusalem, the children bow down before their father or grandfather and receive his blessing; the evening meal is a feast, with all the members of the family united in their festal mood —spiritualised and refined for the time being, whatever their occupations during the week.

As the home is elevated by this fusion, so religion is vitalised by it. Every Jew is expected to be learned in the law; there is no monopoly on the part of the priests; he is bound to know it that he may not transgress. Thus the law itself, when laid down in the Talmud, must enter into all phases of life, and must be kept alive to develop and to embrace the changes of all new conditions of the people. It must take immediate cognisance of daily life with all its ramifications—the house, the market; the duty of citizens, of husbands, of wives, of mothers, of girls and boys; also the duty of man to himself, as affecting his self-respect, his habits of eating and drinking and of cleanliness—in fact, the Talmud enters as nearly as possible into the whole of life. And there can be no doubt that this combination of religion and daily life has had its effect, no only in maintaining higher morality among the Jews, but even in establishing and preserving more refined habits. They certainly were among the first people in Europe who washed regularly. At a time when we know the arrangements for personal cleanliness through-out Europe to have been very imperfect and precarious, it is interesting to read the instruc-tions given by the Spanish Inquisition for recognising and discovering a secret Jew : they turn chiefly upon his habits of eating and drinking, of washing before his meals, of changing his linen on the Sabbath-day.

Of course the danger has been that, whereas in the west of Europe we have advanced in our habits of cleanliness since the romantic Middle Ages, and even within the last fifty years, an orthodox Jew who only adheres to the injunctions of his ancient law might now, by comparison, be on a low stage of cleanli-ness, and that the growth of formalism in their religious injunctions may not have been proof, in all instances, against the degradation which poverty and repression brought upon some communities. No doubt there always was the danger of stereotyping customs into arid formalism, where the religious law, or laws

which partook of some of the weight of religious life, entered into all the nooks and crannies
of daily life.   But there can equally be no
doubt that the fusion not only kept religion
really alive among them, but also directly contributed to the diffusion of culture and learning, besides indirectly refining and elevating
their tastes.   It did this in ever being a source
of education to the people—education of the
elementary and of the higher intellectual
order.   For the Jews never required a Reformation or the invention of the printing-press
to make the Bible known to them.   Most of
the Jews, however humble, could read and
write Hebrew at least, many of them several
other languages.   Even those who have sunk
lowest in Poland and the south-east of Europe
can now read and write their Hebrew characters,
and among them an enormous literature with
extensive publishing establishments exists for
the production of books in Hebrew characters
conveying a patois of German and Hebrew
mixed.[1]   For centuries, while the slender stock
of learning in Europe was in the hands of the
clergy, and the masses of the people, in every

---

[1] Compare the statistics given by Schleiden on this point in
the next chapter.

walk of life, were quite illiterate, the humblest Jews were possessed of the rudiments of education.

But this educating influence of their national and religious life went still further beyond the elementary stages, in that in every small community, even in villages, the men and boys would meet on the Saturday afternoon for Talmudic teaching, learning, and disputation. We need not dwell upon the refining influence it must have had upon the simplest and lowliest people, to be thus in immediate touch with the most abstract thought of a philosophical nature, dwelling upon life actual and spiritual, and all in a most acutely developed logical method, which has had much to do with the sharpening of their intellect. But it went much deeper. Their rabbis could hardly drop into the crass ignorance which stamped some of the clergy; they were, with very few exceptions, deeply learned in Biblical and Talmudic writings; while many young laymen received in these schools a training in philosophic thought which has often set the world wondering when they have once displayed it outside the Jewish circles. The life and history of Spinoza, Moses Mendelssohn, and Solomon

Maimon are striking instances. The latter coming, a poor beggarly boy of thirteen, to Berlin from his low Polish home, was even then a philosopher and dialectician of the first order; and this training he received, not at a university or a theological seminary, but amid the sordid conditions of his wretched Polish village life. The manner in which at the present day the Jews are prominent in the learned professions, in art and science, not only in Germany but throughout Europe, is chiefly due to this continuous tradition of culture among them for so many centuries. But the position which they actually held in the advancement of European culture and civilisation through the Middle Ages, though it has found so able an expositor as the great botanist, the late Professor Schleiden (himself a Christian), is far from being known and appreciated by the most educated and the best-read people among us. I shall devote a special chapter to this subject as treated by Schleiden.

We are now chiefly interested in the bearings upon the refinement of taste which this religious life had for the Jews, taking them as a whole. With the religious functions performed in the homes themselves the more

secular side of the national Jewish life was
kept alive, in that their non-religious Jewish
literature was introduced to even the humblest, and in that the great traditions of the
race were kept before them as a kind of beacon-
light to a more ideal social existence.

To this more secular Jewish literature of the
Middle Ages, down to our times, I shall devote
a special chapter. Its wealth and variety would
again be an object of astonishment to well-read
people in our times.

But what we are concerned with is the fact
that the common people remained familiar with
it—that it became thoroughly domesticated
among them. The lyrical Hebrew songs of the
eleventh, twelfth, thirteenth, and subsequent
centuries were, and are, sung on the Friday
evening, together with the reading of the Bible.
We can easily gauge the refining influence upon
the people, if we were to imagine the modern
Greek peasant reciting to his children, they
joining in, the Homeric poems and the Greek
tragedians, with a real feeling that it was entirely their own; or an English navvy or petty
tradesman reciting Chaucer and Shakespeare
in the family circle, with the sense of its being
essentially their own life. With the Jews we

must add the additional poetic element of the remoteness from the present sordid age. It belonged to their golden age. They ever sang of Jerusalem, that star of idealism glimmering brightly in their distant past, but showing the way to a nobler and fairer future.

They felt that, let their oppressors and despisers do and say what they would, they, the peddlers and toilers, were still the chosen people. This produced the self-contained, inner, spiritual pride, unostentatious in its glow by their own hearth, the very opposite of the plebeian *parvenu's* pride, which is directed to the gallery, and lives by the support and admiration of the mass who admire mean things. It is the pride which characterises the self-centred nobility of a truly aristocratic nature.

And this has also produced a chivalry. It is a mistake to think that in their dispersion the Jews have always suffered misery and persecution. When we read the catalogue of their cruel sufferings the impression is one of continuous torture; but we must never forget that if history records the series of wars, it does not in the same way give due proportion to the periods of intervening prosperity and growth of culture and happiness. Nay, if we were merely to record the wars in our century, from the Napoleonic wars through the Revolution of 1848, the Crimean, the American Civil War, the Italian, Danish, Prusso-Austrian, Franco-Prussian, Russo-Turkish wars, and the minor wars and disturbances, the reader of our history some time hence would hardly realise that there was time and space for all the glorious advancement in art and science, for the growth of civilisation and culture, which so brightly stamp our age. So, too, the period of martyrdom of the Jews in the Middle Ages and the subsequent centuries was relieved by centuries of prosperity and culture in which the yoke of the oppressor was not felt; then, by the side of their literature and science, a high chivalrous life and character were developed. Especially among the Spanish Jews do we find chivalrous and polite dignity. We can see Rabbi Astruc de Porta drawing himself up, in answering De Peñaforte, the Dominican persecutor, who enjoined upon him not to use the liberty of discussion to slander Christianity, when in 1263 King Jayme called him and other Jews to defend their faith against Christianity, ' I, too, know the rules of courtesy.'

As to their pluck and courage, it certainly did not die out with the Maccabees and the Zealots. I will not mention the spiritual courage it required for the whole race to survive at all during the persecutions which might have been avoided by the simple act of conversion, or of the thousands that burned at the stake singing—I should say even numerically more than the whole Christian martyrology has to show. The numbers who heroically during the Spanish Inquisition, and at other times and places, preferred burning at the stake to baptism, the perfidy which often met their heroic resistance would fill volumes. In the history of the Spanish Jews more than in that of any other of their numerous communities do we meet with heroism, courage, and chivalry. They fought in the Spanish battles as the bravest knights. Alphonso X. of Castile rewarded them *en masse* for their warlike assistance against Seville, and gave them, when the enemy's land was divided, a village which was called Aldea de los Judeos. They fought desperately for Don Pedro, even after the Black Prince had forsaken him, defended Burgos to the last man, so that even their opponent, Don Enrico, recognised publicly their valour. But even in Germany, during the Black Death and the butchery of Jews, and in Poland, the spirit of the Maccabees and the Zealots had not forsaken them. It very often met with the basest treachery on the part of their enemies and allies. One instance is a striking, if not a typical, one. During the onslaught of the Cossacks into Poland in the Thirty Years' War the Jews were brave defenders of the Polish territory. When a horde of Hadamaks attacked the town of Tulczyn, six thousand Christians and about two thousand Jews retreated to the fortress. Nobles and Jews pledged themselves by oath to defend the fortress to the last man. The Cossacks resorted to a stratagem, and assured the nobles that they were only fighting against their real enemies, the Jews. If these were handed over to them they would withdraw. The nobles asked the Jews to give them their arms; and when they complied, they opened the gates to the Cossacks. When the Cossacks had plundered the Jews they proposed to them the alternative of death or baptism. Not one of them accepted the latter, and they were put to the sword. But the nobles suffered the same fate, for the Cossacks held that there was no cause to keep faith with the faithless. In more modern times many instances of fortitude like the one recently published of a New York merchant might be adduced. Professor Cyrus Adler quotes from an unpublished letter of Jared Sparks: 'At the outbreak of the Revolutionary War a Mr. Gomez, of New York, proposed to a member of the Continental Congress that he form a company of soldiers for service. The member of Congress remonstrated with Mr. Gomez on the score of age, he then being sixty-eight years of age, to which Mr. Gomez replied "that he could stop a bullet as well as a younger man."'

If we look into the position they held collectively as a people, and the esteem they won for themselves, we shall find that they can well bear comparison with any other body of people in modern history. The climax of their life was reached in Spain; but we shall see that all through the Middle Ages, and since the Reformation, in other countries too, they held a position which was far from being degraded; while intellectually and morally they may claim to have stood highest.

An interesting episode is the history of the Kingdom of the Chazari or Kozari. They were a warlike race of the Finnish tribe, related to the Bulgarians and Hungarians, and settled on the border between Asia and Europe. Near Astrachan they had founded an empire at the mouth of the Volga. They overran Persia, crossed the Caucasus, and made inroads into Armenia, conquering the Crimean peninsula, which for some time was called after them Chazaria. The Byzantine emperors stood in great fear of them, lest they should be tempted to conquer Constantinople, and paid them a tribute. Several nations, including the Bulgarians, were their vassals, and the Russians on the Dnieper (the irony of history?) had to present them with one sword and a fur for every chimney.

In the eighth century their king, Bulan or Butshan, adopted Judaism, together with his court and the whole aristocracy. Under one of his successors, Obadja, the moral influence of Judaism really made itself felt. He invited learned Jews to settle among his people, founded schools and synagogues, which greatly contributed to their civilisation. There is a long line of rulers after Obadja, all of Jewish faith (for the king could only be chosen from this faith) but manifesting perfect tolerance

to those in their country who had not adopted
Judaism, and who had equal rights with the
Jews.   I think it not impossible that many of
the Jews now expelled from the south of Russia
are descendants of this people—and perhaps
also a number of Russian orthodox Christians.

If we begin by considering the Jewish
people as a whole during the Middle Ages we
must first cast our eyes to the East, while at
a very early period the intellectual leadership
is transferred to the West.

With the spread of Arabian culture under
the Caliphate of Bagdad, the Jews were intimately concerned.   From the time of Haroun
Alraschid and his son Almamum, the Jewish
rabbis and schoolmen took an active part in
the science and learning of the day, which was
much higher in the East than it was during the
same period in Europe.   As the intellectual
and religious life of the Jews was in those
days centred in the great schools of Babylon,
and then of Sura and Pumbadita, their social
life had as its recognised head the prince of
exile, or the exilarch, as he was called, who
resided at Bagdad, and was recognised as the
chief of all Jews, until the social as well as

intellectual leadership was transferred to Spain. These exilarchs were very important personages in the caliph's empire, and were recognised as such by the rulers, and much esteemed by them. They often, we may say generally, combined the position of religious and scientific teacher with that of their political and social leadership—a combination which, throughout the whole of the Jewish history, was customary. Both these functions of the exilarch were accompanied with great pomp and ceremony. So, for instance, we are told that Samuel Bar Ali Halevi sat on a throne, clad in gold and embroidery, with two thousand disciples at his feet. And in the same way he administered justice with his nine assessors beside him. In the twelfth century the Caliph Almuktafi restored to the office of exilarch its former brilliancy, permitted them to live in princely splendour, to wear a turban of honour, to ride surrounded by a guard of honour, and to have an official seal. When the exilarch appeared in public or approached the caliph, a herald preceded him, shouting, ' Make room for our lord, the son of David.'

But besides the Jews dwelling under the caliphate, there were independent Jewish nationalities in the East. So in the country Aserbeidsan there was a warlike tribe of Jews who at one time, under David Alruchi (Alroy), had a history full of enterprise and adventure. There was also an independent warlike tribe of Jews in the District Chorasan, in the moun-tains near Nishabur. In the twelfth century there were many Jews living as far as Khiva and Samarcand. A large number also dwelt in Arabia about this time, and especially in North Arabia, where there were independent tribes, with their own princes and citadels, thoroughly able to take care of themselves. We shall examine later the position the Jews held in Turkey after their expulsion from Spain and Portugal.

If we turn to Europe, in which we are chiefly interested, the Jews, as we have already seen, were settled there as early as Roman times, and lived on terms of perfect equality with all their neighbours, until religious intol-erance set itself to repress them, or directed and intensified the jealousy which their suc-cess elicited. When the west of Europe was raised out of its barbarism by Charlemagne, this great leader of modern civilisation also took account of the valuable civilising influence

of the Jews, especially as regarded commerce
and learning. He granted them privileges,
and even made use of them for diplomatic
services ; and as he transplanted learned men
from Italy into France and Germany in order
that their wisdom might be diffused among his
subjects, so he also desired to engraft the
learning of the Jews in these districts. He
encouraged them to found Talmudic schools ;
he transplanted from Lucca the learned family
Kalonymos to Narbonne about the year 787,
gave them a large tract of land in the town,
where the chief of the family and his successors were called princes, while the part of the
town where they lived was called 'The Court
of the King of the Jews.' The position which
the Jew Isaac held in the embassy of Charlemagne to Haroun Alraschid is a matter of history. The son and successor of Charlemagne,
Louis, showered favours upon the Jews, and
his wife Judith had the greatest enthusiasm
for the ancient Jewish heroes. Even in the
eleventh and twelfth centuries in France and
Germany the Jews were still free possessors
of land, had their vineyards, were artisans and
merchants. Until the time of the Crusades,
both in France and Germany, they lived in

comfort, and even in great affluence. They
were rich in land and in town property. It
was said that the greater part of Paris belonged
to them. It was only when the kings needed
money that they occasionally persecuted them
in order to rob them of what they possessed.
In the south of France, Marseilles, Beziers,
Montpellier, Posquières, in the whole of
Languedoc and Provence, at Narbonne, Lunel,
Toulouse, Bourg de St. Gilles, there were
wealthy and thriving communities, with independent internal jurisdiction, and with rich
culture flowing from their flourishing rabbinic
schools. The same applied to the north of
France, to Germany, Austria, and Silesia. In
the latter state they possessed several villages
down to the twelfth century. Worms, Mayence, Cologne, Frankfort were great centres,
where even in the twelfth century they carried
arms and were admitted to duels, where they
fought bravely with their Christian brethren
against any common foe. Wise princes often
stemmed the tide of fanaticism and jealousy
by confirming their privileges or adding to
them. So the Duke Leopold of Austria, the
contemporary of Richard Cœur de Lion; and
so the Emperor Frederick II. (in spite of his

inconsistent treatment of them) recognised
their civilising influence, corresponded with
some of their wise men, and invited them to
come and reside at Naples. So also the Arch-
duke Frederick I. of Austria, in the thirteenth
century, made several of them high officials,
and bestowed titles upon them. He protected
them against the attacks of their enemies, and
made special laws in their favour.

In Italy and in the Papal States, owing to
the friendliness which the Pope Alexander III.
had for them, down to the end of the twelfth
century, they were unhampered in their free
development. This era produced great poets,
who were certainly in touch, if not in communication, with Dante, and ought to be
studied by all those who read the greatest
Italian poet and are concerned with the history
of civilisation in this period. So also in the
south of Italy and in Sicily they flourished
unhampered, and the Normans Roger II. and
William II. confirmed their privileges.

Before their banishment from England,
under Edward I., the Jews had been very
prosperous—so prosperous that, no doubt, their
wealth, coupled with religious fanaticism, was
the cause of the terrible persecutions and

massacres which they experienced subsequently at York, Northampton, Exeter, Lynn, Norwich, and other towns. Under Henry II. their position was an excellent one. Many of them had great palaces in London, in York, and in other cities, and there were large numbers of Christians who looked with such favour upon their religion that they became converted to it, so that there was a congregation consisting only of such converts.

In the east of Europe, in Bohemia, Moravia, and Poland, they began to be conspicuous in the tenth century. The community of Prague is perhaps one of the oldest in Europe, and of much earlier date than the tenth century; but it was certainly flourishing in that time, when the apostle to the Prussians, Woytech Adalbert, formerly Archbishop of Prague, was disturbed in his dreams because so many Christians were the servants of the Jews. These Jews of Prague were an independent body, possessed of great wealth. In Moravia there were also Jews of importance, one of whom built a castle bearing his name (Podiva). In the eleventh century there were Jews in the kingdom of Poland, especially in the capital, Gnesen, where they were not forbidden to

K

have Christian slaves.   Under Casimir IV.,
the privileges which originally Boteslaw, and
then Casimir the Great, had granted them,
and which were considerable, were confirmed
by Casimir IV., and even increased.   The Jews
in Poland in those days supplied the class of
the *bourgeoisie*, as there were then only nobles
and serfs in that country.

But the brilliant centre of Jewish life
in the Middle Ages, down to the end of the
fifteenth century, is to be found in Spain.

We have already seen that there were important and flourishing Jewish communities
in the Iberian peninsula from the earliest
times; but it was not until the tenth century
that they began to hold that prominent social
and intellectual position which they maintained there for about five centuries, and after
their expulsion carried with them to other
countries.   Their own moral and social superiority in Spain is coincident with the superiority in culture of this country under the
Moors over all the rest of Europe.   It was
under Abd-ul-Rhaman III. that Spain became
the one country in Europe that was a real seat
of learning and art.   As about this time the
great seats of Jewish life and thought in the

East—Pumbadita and Sura—lost in their
influence, the torch was handed on from these
places to Spain, with Cordova as the first
centre. Moses Ben Chanoch found his way
from Sura to Cordova, and thus was an immediate link between the Eastern school and
that of the West; while the great personality
of Chasdai Ibn Shaprut, the wealthy philosopher, statesman, and ambassador, the patron of
all sciences and arts, really gave active life to
the flower of Hebrew culture in that country.
Not only Talmudic studies were developed to
the highest degree, but also the sciences, philosophy, philology, together with the culture
of the muses which led to the production of
that rich Neo-Hebraic poetry, of the wealth of
which but few people have an adequate idea.
The political and social position of the Jews
in this country and during these five hundred
years was also so brilliant that no doubt
it contributed much towards fanning that
animosity which resulted in their cruel persecution and expulsion. We shall look into some
of the individual cases manifesting this high
social position; yet if we attempt to convey
a picture of the life and surroundings of the
distinguished Jews of those days, the ignorant

modern anti-Semite would find it difficult to
reconcile it with his conception of the Old-
clothes Jew.   He could hardly imagine the
distinguished Jew of the day, in the tenth
century, passing through the streets of Cordova, accompanied by eighteen pages, and
driving in a carriage of state, as Jacob Ibn Gau
was wont to do.   He could not easily realise
the picture conveyed by the description which
the great Abrabanel gives of his life in Portugal before his expulsion at the close of the
fifteenth century : ' Peaceably I lived in my
father's house in the far-famed Lisbon, and
God had given me there many blessings,
wealth, and honour.   I had built great edifices
and vast halls, my house was a centre for the
learned and the wise.   I was beloved in the
palace of Alphonso, a mighty and just king,
under whom the Jews were free and enjoyed
prosperity.   I was closely tied to him ; he
leant upon me, and as long as he lived I
freely entered the palace.'

But with these splendid surroundings, what
really brought honour among the Jews were
learning and a lofty character.   Rabbis and
teachers did not receive pay.   The esteem
which the possession of money in itself brings,

I maintain, was less prominent among them than with other people, and only began to take hold among the Jews when through the downfall of feudalism and with the French Revolution, money became such a source of power in the whole of Europe. The Jews were then affected by this general current of European history. I do not mean to say that, as merchants and workers, they did not always desire to be successful in their endeavours to gain wealth, especially as it was the one means, together with their learning, of gaining power in the outer world. But money, in the early times, did not carry with it distinction among themselves, and was not looked upon as the highest good. Their teachers and moral leaders were those most respected, and were received with a reverence which others gave to princes and kings. But often the great and wealthy were also the wisest and the best. The great families in Spain really had an effective *noblesse oblige*; they were all trained in the same schools, and sought for distinction by intellectual superiority. Nay, I venture to hold that the efficient causes which led to their success in life through the acquisition of wealth and power, as merchants, financiers

or physicians, were immediately the same as
those which made them learned and wise. The
theoretical and practical were not dissociated in
Talmudic and rabbinic teaching. The Talmud
comprised the wisdom of life, and the Talmudic
disputations sharpened their dialectic sense.
I even venture to think that the clear-headed-
ness, the critical power and sharpness of intellect, which characterises the Jews in our time,
is in some measure due to the continuous
practice in their Talmudic disputations; and
it may be possible that this habit of mind has
been in some form or other transmitted by
heredity as a general mental quality. At all
events I would call upon the reader to picture
to himself a worldly aristocracy, who were at
the same time the leaders in thought and art,
and to imagine the whole people taking active
interest or part in the discussion of high subjects. He will then have an adequate idea of
the true spirit of Jewish life in Spain during the
Middle Ages—and, for that, in later periods
too, down to many instances in modern times.

Grouping round Ibn Shaprut there were a
number of poets and philosophers, such as
Charisi, Menahem Ben Saruk, and Dunash
Ben Labrat. The position of Ibn Shaprut in

the outer world, too, was a great one. He was practically minister of foreign affairs to his country, and took an important part in the historical embassies which were sent—the one by the Byzantine emperor, Constantine VIII., the other by the German emperor, Otho I.—to the Court of Cordova. Among the Spanish Jews there were families who formed a kind of aristocracy — but always an aristocracy based upon intellectual and moral superiority. Such were the Ibn Esras, the Alfachars, Ibn Faljags, Ibn Giats, Benvenistes, Ibn Migashs, Abulafias, and others. The prominent men among them who had gained great political influence made good their claim by being themselves great thinkers, or men of science, or poets, and were nearly always men of the noblest character. The centres of culture and refinement in this period, besides Cordova, were Lucena and Granada.

In the eleventh century not only did literature and philology reach its climax among them, but also philosophy reached its highest point under Maimonides. The long line of poets culminates in Yehuda-Ben-Halevi.

Under Ali in Spain, in the first half of the twelfth century, the Jews also held great

political positions; several of them were viziers
and ambassadors, while nearly all these were
at the same time scientific men, generally
physicians, and were learned in their own law.
The rabbis themselves were either poets or
protectors of poetry.

After this period, with the second crusade,
occasional persecutions began, and these grew
as the Catholic clergy gained power and
opposed themselves to the prominence of the
Jews.   But as in Germany, with its numerous
principalities, so here, the repressions were
only local and temporary, and at no time
previous to their expulsion did they fail to
maintain their position in Spain.

When Cordova falls from its height, Toledo
becomes the great centre, and through the influence of Ibn Esra, a prince by position, commander of Callatrava, the fate of the Jews
was a very happy one.   Here in the second half
of the twelfth century, under Alphonso VIII.,
the congregation numbered 12,000 members.
They erected beautiful synagogues, and they
were not only wealthy and cultured, but also
brave warriors.   The young men, skilled in the
use of arms, took part in the tournaments.

There   was   one   fundamental   difficulty,

which was the cause of much of their misfortune, namely, that while on the one
hand they were too independent and powerful to be completely subjected by the state
in which they lived, they could still not form
a separate state of their own.   This was perhaps the political difficulty which made
many of the persecutions possible.   As a
body they thus only had part in local politics,
and often thus stood fighting against one
another; and as an historical necessity they
often were crushed between the two contending parties.   So 40,000 of them fought against
Alphonso VI. in black and yellow turbans,
while there were many Jews on his side.
They also fought valiantly for Alphonso VIII.
in 1195.

In Aragon and Catalonia, under Alphonso
II., in the second half of the twelfth century,
they were also powerful and flourishing,
especially the communities of Barcelona, Tudela,
and Gerona.   Even in the thirteenth century,
with Nachmani and his family as their intellectual leaders, they flourished, though
life and thought and poetry seemed from this
time to flow here in thinner streams.

In the second half of the thirteenth century,

under Alphonso x. of Castile, in whose army against Seville many Jews fought, great concessions were made to them, and at his court there were Jews in high office. The same power was given them by Ferdinand IV., in the first half of the fourteenth century; while the regent Don Juan Emmanuel also showed himself their good friend and again employed some in important state offices.

So also in the south of Spain, in Castile, they prospered in this period, and their position became strengthened under Alphonso XI. But under his son, Don Pedro of Castile, their influence in this country grew greater than at any other time. His own private counsellor, an all-powerful man in the state, was Don Samuel Ben Meir Alavi, and other Jews also held important positions at the court. The favour which Don Pedro showed the Jews was so great that he was called a Jew by his enemies. His brother Henry, his successful rival, rewarded rather than punished the Jews for their faithfulness to their king, his enemy. Though he protected them against the people who began to chafe under the power of the Jews, he could not entirely stem the current of animosity; and soon, in the year 1391, the cruel and systematic persecutions began which reached their height in the Inquisition of Torquemada.

The persecutions at the end of the fourteenth century and in the subsequent periods of course led to frequent forced conversions to Christianity. The result was that the social position of the Jews was for the time being bettered rather than repressed. But this again led to more barbarous persecutions than before; for it is natural that those who thus became Christians, possessed of superior wealth and intellectual power, again attained the highest positions, while they were still connected by blood, and generally by affection and sympathy, with the Jews of their own families. Thus many great families, like the De la Caballaria, were partly Christian and partly Jewish. These new Christians or Marranos formed a third party of enormous power and influence, and it was against them that the Inquisition was chiefly directed. A large number of the great noble families of Spain of the present day are of Jewish extraction; and it is perhaps owing to his intimate acquaintance with Spanish history and literature (for upon the latter also the Jewish-Spanish poets had considerable influence) that Mr. Lowell was first led to his theory which we have quoted above.

But even in the fifteenth century the Jews themselves had not lost their high standing, in spite of the Inquisition. So, under Juan II., especially through the influence of Abraham Ben Veniste, who stood high with him, the Jews began to recover for a short time from the blows which had been struck at them. In Aragon, also, the king's counsellor, Juan de Pacheco (though of Jewish extraction, himself an enemy of the Jews), could not forego the help of the powerful Ben Veniste family.

At first, under Ferdinand and Isabella (the former of whom, it was said, had Jewish blood in his veins), the new Christians Don Pedro De la Caballaria and the Jew Don Abraham Senior had considerable influence.

The last of the long line of the Jewish statesmen was Don Isaac Abrabanel, who worthily closes the history of their sojourn in Spain for so many centuries. For at the close of the fifteenth century these earliest and most cultured of the inhabitants of the Spanish Peninsula were expelled from their home.

In Portugal the same fate befell them,

though a few years later than in Spain. Here their position had been equally brilliant. The Jews of Portugal had a complete organisation, they stood under the rabbi-chief who had almost the power of a prince. He had a special seal, was chief-judge, and signed documents in the name of the king. Once a year he travelled on inspection over the whole country, accompanied by a chief-judge (*quividor*), a chancellor, a secretary (*escrivao*), and an executive officer (*porteiro jurado*). There were seven rabbis (*ouvidores*) in the several provinces. They had supreme power under the chief rabbi in their provinces, and had jurisdiction in civil as well as criminal law. Don Ferdinand, king of Portugal, had a Jew, Don Judah, as his minister of finance (*tesoreiro mor*), and Don David Negro as a privy-councillor.

The banishment of these Spanish and Portuguese Jews from the homes of their fathers, and the description of these men of high character—gentlemen in the true sense of the word—wandering all over the earth in search of a home, is one of the most painful chapters in history. But wherever they went they took their culture with them, and as their expulsion from Spain is coincident with the decline of the prosperity in that country, so their emigration into Holland and Hamburg, and even England, is coincident with the rise of prosperity in those countries.

But it is a mistake to believe that, with the dispersion of the Jews of Spain, their social position and refinement were entirely destroyed. Even after that, as a body and as individuals, they were still possessed of great distinction.

Many of the families expelled from Spain and Portugal found refuge in Italy, where, in the fifteenth century, the Jews were highly prosperous. The commerce of Venice, Florence, Genoa, and Pisa in the fifteenth and sixteenth centuries made it desirable that some of the capital possessed by the Jews should be attracted there. Among them men like Jechiel of Pisa, were very prominent as financiers in Tuscany. As physicians, too, they held high and influential positions, such as that of Guglielmo di Portaleone, of Mantua, who was the court-physician to Ferdinand of Naples and to Galeazzo Sforza. The intercourse with their Christian fellow-citizens was hearty. The picture of the wedding feast at the marriage of the daughter of the wealthy Leo of Crema, where Christians and

Jews danced and feasted together for eight days, is an instance of this. Some of the first printing-presses at Reggio, Mantua, Ferrara, Pieva di Sacco, Bologna, Soncino, Iscion, and Naples were started by Jews. Though, owing to the strictures of their religion, they were not allowed to become painters or sculptors, and thus did not contribute materially to the artistic revival in the Renaissance, they did much to foster the scientific revival in Italy more directly through such men as Messer Leon, the rabbi, physician, Latin scholar, and Aristotelian philosopher of Mantua, and Elia del Medigo or Elia Cretensis, the teacher of Pico di Mirandola.[1]

In the sixteenth century, under Alexander VI., Julius II., Leo X., and Clement VII., they maintained their position in Italy. Most of these popes had Jewish physicians; while in the north of Italy, at the Court of Ferrara, at Lecce, at Perugia, at Padova, and Ancona, and many other cities, there were many influential Jews. Pope Paul III. was so favourable to them that the Bishop of Carpentras wrote :

[1] The next chapter will contain the researches of Professor Schleiden on this subject. But it was necessary to mention a few instances in this general survey.

'Christians have never received as many favours, privileges, and concessions as the Jews receive from Paul III. They have not only been advanced with distinctions and favours, but they have even been armed with them.' The same was done towards the close of the century by Sixtus V. In the seventeenth century there were still distinguished and wealthy families, especially at Livorno and Florence.

Another large party of these refugees from Spain and Portugal went to Turkey, where they gained for themselves high positions. This was especially the case with the physicians, who found great favour under Sultan Selim and his successors in the sixteenth century. The Jews had their own political representative, Kahiji, as he was called, who had free access to the Sultan, and protected their interests. In the second half of the sixteenth century their position grew still better in Turkey, when through the family of the Nassi, and especially Don Joseph, Duke of Naxos, the Jews became a real political power.

The most important body settled in Holland, chiefly in Amsterdam. Thither, at the beginning of the seventeenth century, the centre of Jewish life was transferred from Spain. Many of the Marranos, Neo-Christians from Spain, had settled here, and had returned to Judaism; and there grew up a community with distinguished members in all walks of life. There were statesmen, poets, men of science, and merchants, forming not only a centre for their religious life, but also for higher culture and an extended commerce, through which the trade of Holland no doubt attained its vast proportions. Nor must it be believed that this community, which produced its Spinoza, who seceded from it, had not among the members remaining true to it a large number of highly intellectual people of all shades of thought. It even received into its body men like Vicente de Rocamora, who had previously been confessor to the Infanta Maria, subsequently the Empress of Germany. The list of distinguished names among this community in the seventeenth century is a long one, and the work of their poets is worthy of a serious monograph. In 1675, when there numbered 4000 families in Amsterdam, they built a splendid synagogue, for the inauguration of which Romein de Hooghe wrote a poem, and for the erection of which Christians had advanced money.

Another mass of the Portuguese Jews settled at Hamburg, and with their advent the prosperity of that city began. Of the bank of Hamburg, founded about 1620, twelve of these Portuguese Jews were the originators; and these families, the Lopes, Brandons, Abandanas, the Da Limas, the Cardosos, the Texeiras, and others, have been among the most prominent citizens of the great merchant city.

At Bordeaux also there were and are still ancient families of Jewish extraction who held and hold prominent position as merchants.

In England, Cromwell showed great preference for the Jewish faith, a preference which marked all the Puritans, and it is about this time that the Jewish merchants often supposed to be Lombards, again settled in London, where, before that time, men like Lopes, Carvagal, Robles, Mendes, and others, had been settled, though not known to be Jews. They would meet, to avoid disturbance, in the chapel of the Portuguese ambassador, Antonio de Souza, the father-in-law of Carvagal, which really was converted into a synagogue. But it was not until the return of Charles II. that

the merchants from Amsterdam were allowed to
settle openly in England, where their activity
accrued to the benefit of English commerce.

With the close of the seventeenth century
the intellectual life of the Jews seems to have
declined, owing to the general course of
European history, as well as to the degeneracy
of their own rabbinical work during this period.
The revival of their intellectual and moral life
we must look for in Germany.   This revival of
refinement we find at first in the north of Germany, especially at Berlin, where the personality of Moses Mendelssohn played no small
part in the raising of the intellectual standard
for the whole of Germany, but especially for
that of the Jewish world.   From this time on
Berlin became a centre of the highest culture
—literary, scientific, and social.   It is difficult
to convey in a few words the picture of the
refinement which existed among the wealthy
and prominent Jewish families of Berlin during
the second half of the eighteenth and the first
half of the nineteenth centuries.   Though one
may not always approve of the tone of the
salons of many of the wealthy amateurs of this
capital, there is abundance of proof to show
that they stood out in the city as most attrac-

tive to those who sought for social ease and intellectual refinement. From that day on the Jews in Germany have taken up the light of the education which prevails in that country, and have mixed in, and contributed to, its intellectual advancement (not to speak of its commercial and industrial welfare) as have no other body of men which we can single out among the constituent factors of the German Empire.

I have roughly sketched the general position which the Jews have held in Europe from the Middle Ages on; but the impression I wish to convey would be imperfect if I did not attempt, by singling out some of the prominent individuals, to give an idea of the brighter side of the social position they occupied for these many centuries. It is difficult to make such a list at all complete, especially as so many of the prominent Jews and Jewish families became converted, and were forced by physical or moral pressure to hide their origin. And, again, there are many prominent men with mixed Jewish blood in their veins; and though a mother may have had the greater share in producing or educating a man of genius and note, she does not so manifestly stand before

the eyes of history.   So, for instance, it is not
generally known that the mother of Montaigne
was Antoinette de Louppes, the daughter of
Pedro Lopes, a Spanish Jew; and there are
no doubt numerous cases of this kind of which
history has no record.   It is furthermore a
mistake to believe that the influence which the
Jews attained was due to their money.   I
think it was equally, or even in a greater
measure, due to their intellectual and moral
qualities, which made themselves felt often in
conjunction with their wealth, as well as to the
fact that, for several centuries, they were the
real students of science in Europe.   As
physicians they were sought for by the great
of the land all over the world, so that even the
popes who issued bulls against them and
forbade them to pursue the practice of medicine
would only intrust their bodies to the care of
Jewish physicians.   It is greatly through this
practice of medicine that many of them
attained the influential positions in the world
which they occupied.[1]

[1] I have heard physicians in Germany and elsewhere com-
plain that the Jews were encroaching upon the profession of
medicine.   If the Jews were weak enough to fear ordinary
emulation and competition, and were foolish and narrow-
hearted enough to express their fear, they might with greater
historical justice consider the others as intruders into a

In this more detailed and personal examination of the position of the Jews, many prominent men may be omitted, while names and families may be repeated which have already been touched upon in the more general treatment I have just given.

We begin the record with the times of Charlemagne, and we have here already mentioned the family Kalonymos, who at Narbonne bore the title of Princes (Nassi) down to the period of the expulsion of the Jews from France. A branch of this family was at the same time also settled at Mayence.

Under the same monarch a Jew named Isaac was attached, in 797, to the embassy sent to Haroun-Al-Rashid, at first probably only an interpreter; but after the death of Llandfried and Sigismund he returned from the East as the chief. Under Louis the Pious, in the tenth century, we hear of a nobleman and priest named Bodo, a member of an old Allemanian family, who left the Church and became converted to Judaism, and settled in Spain under the name of Eliazar in the year 938.

domain which had been specially their own for centuries in the whole of Europe, and for the development of which science they have ever done and are now doing more than their share.

Under Charles the Bold there were two prominent Jews attached to his court: the one, Zedekiah, was his court physician; the other, Judah, stood in high favour with him, and was called by him the 'faithful one.' In the eleventh century, Semon Ben Abum, of Mayence, was a man far famed for his wealth, learning, and charitable character.

In the twelfth century, in the south of France, we have as another brilliant figure the Princess Ermengarde Kalonymos Ben Trodros, a descendant of those Jews planted there by Charlemagne. The family of the Kimchi were here celebrated as philosophers and students. At Beziers, in this period, Moses de Cavarite and Nathan were administrators to Viscount Roger, the friend of the Albigenses. Towards the close of the twelfth century we also find a certain Solomon as the financial adviser to Duke Leopold of Austria, celebrated for his connection with Richard Cœur de Lion.

How thoroughly the Jews were nationalised in this period is illustrated by the fact that a certain Suezkint of Trimberg (a town in Saxony) was a German minnesinger, writing in the style of his contemporaries, Walter von der Vogelweide and Wolfram von Eschenbach.

The financial adviser of Pope Alexander III. was a certain Jechiel Ben Abraham, of the family of the Dei Mansi, a nephew of the Nathan Dei Mansi who wrote a Talmudic lexicon.

Of the prosperity of the Jews in England I have already spoken. Foremost among these was, perhaps, Aaron of York; while a certain Benedict and another Joceus of the same city were forcibly converted to Christianity.

In the thirteenth century the brothers Leblin and Nekelo were two out of several to whom titles were given, and they were known officially as counts and chamberlains of the Duke of Austria.

If now we turn to Spain, we find in the tenth century the prominent figure, whom we have already met, Chasdai Ben Isaac Ibn Shaprut, of the family of Ibn Ezra, born 915 and died 970. He is a thoroughly European figure, combining grace with his deeper moral and intellectual qualities. His father Isaac was wealthy and generous, and a patron of arts and sciences, and thus influenced the direction of taste in his son, who began to study medicine and philology. He was not only a thorough master of Hebrew and Arabic, but also a good

Latin Scholar. In 941 he was made interpreter and diplomatic agent to Abd-ul-Rahman
III., and became the leading diplomat. I have
already mentioned the two important embassies
in which he was concerned. At the same time,
also, he encouraged culture among the Jews,
and thus there grouped round him a number
of shining lights in science and art, such as
Menahem Ben Saruc, Dunash Ben Labrat,
and others.

A very remarkable personality among the
Jews in Spain in the eleventh century was
Samuel Ibn Nagrela. He was a patron of
science and art, a poet and writer deeply
learned in Talmudic lore. He at first became
private secretary to Ibn Alarif, Vizir of King
Habus of Granada, and when his chief was
taken ill he was made minister of state (*catir*),
and had in his hand the diplomatic affairs of
the kingdom. In spite of his enemies, he was
for thirty years the practical ruler of the kingdom, living in the palace of the king. Badis,
the successor of Habus, confirmed him in his
position, though his enemies nearly succeeded
in bringing about his fall.

There is extant an Arabian poem by a
Mohammedan in which the high merits of this

prominent Jew are sung. He was succeeded
in all his positions and dignities by his son
Abu Hussain Joseph. The beginning of his
loss of favour with King Badis shows the
courage of the man. The king had formed
a terrible resolve, to slay all the Arab population in his capital, and Joseph did all in his
power to dissuade him from this resolution.
But Badis stuck to his purpose, and gave the
orders to his officers. Then Joseph sent word
to the chief Arabs, begging them not to go to
the mosque on the coming Friday; and when
the soldiers of the king entered, they found
chiefly Barbs and only a few old Arabs, and
could not carry out the king's diabolical plan.
Enraged, the king charged Joseph with having
betrayed his secret; and Joseph said freely
that the king ought to thank God that he had
saved him from this great danger. 'The time
will come,' he said, 'when you will share my
views and approve of the counsel I have given
you.' Though the king forgave him, still the
sting remained, and soon Joseph fell a victim
to his enemies. Joseph was not so learned as
his father, who, besides being a poet in seven
languages, wrote a new psalter, a book of
sayings and sermons, and corresponded with

all the learned men in the East.   There were
other learned prominent men about this time,
such as Ibn Garnach (Jona Marinus) and the
great poet Ibn Gebirol.

Alphonso VI. of Castile also had as one of
his chief diplomats and ambassadors Amram
Ibn Shalbib, at one time his court physician,
and afterwards his ambassador to the various
courts.   Another counsellor in state affairs was
a Jew named Cidelus.   Ibn Shalbib lost his
life in service ; for when, accompanied by five
hundred knights, he went as the king's ambassador to Seville, Almutammed was so incensed
at the demands which he conveyed to him, that,
against all custom, he slew the ambassador.

This King Almutammed had as his astronomer a Jew Ibn Albalia, who was at the same
time the chief of the Jewish community in
the principality of Seville.   His Talmudic
opponent was the celebrated Isaac Alfassi.
This enmity ended in a very touching episode.
When Albalia's son Baruch was weeping at his
death-bed, the dying father charged him that
he was to go after his death to his enemy
Alfassi at Lucena, and convey to him his
words : that at death's door he forgave Alfassi
all that he, by word of mouth or in writing,

had said against him, that he expected Alfassi would also forgive him, and that he hoped that Alfassi would welcome the son of his enemy. The son followed his father's commands, and Alfassi embraced him with tears, saying to him: 'I shall henceforth be thy father,' and he lived up to his promise.

In the twelfth century a Jewish poet and physician, Solomon Ibn Almuallem, of Seville, was court physician to the Caliph Ali, and bore the title Prince and Vizir. Ibn Kamnial of Saragossa held the same title. He was also a physician and a man of very noble character, of whom all the poets of his day sang. Another prominent prince of the time was Ibn Farussal. He was probably in the service of some Christian ruler in Spain, and was sent as ambassador to the court of Murcia. The astronomer Ben Chija Albar Geloni, about the same time, also bore the title of Prince and held the office of Chief of Police, as we might call him (*Zachib as Schorta*).

The most prominent family of Granada in this period were the four brothers Ibn Esra, of ancient lineage, wealthy, and gifted with great talents. They were all four men of letters, but the greatest among them was the poet Moses Ibn Esra. But he, of course, was outshone by the great poetic light of this age, Jehuda Ben Halevi. The son of one of these brothers Ibn Esra—Jehuda Ibn Esra—stood high in favour with King Alphonso Raimundez in the twelfth century. When Ibn Esra conquered the fortress Calatravas, on the boundary between Toledo and Cordova, the emperor made him commander of the fortress, and conferred upon him the title of Prince. In 1149 he was made marshal of the king's court. Of the culture of Toledo in this period I have already spoken. With such men as Abraham Ibn Daud and Abraham Ibn Esra, learning and poetry flourished here as never before. Under Alphonso VIII., Joseph Ben Salamo Ibn Shoshan was also called Prince, and stood very close to his king, as did also Abraham Ibn Alfachar.

In Aragon and Catalonia Sheshet Ben Veniste, a physician and poet, was also in the diplomatic service of Alphonso II., and is praised for his support of learning and science. Next to him at Barcelona was Samuel Ibn Chasdai Halevi, a prominent and learned man. He had five sons, all of whom were men of distinction; of them one is chiefly known as a translator of philosophical works, and the writer of a romance or novel called *The Prince and the Dervish*. In the same period Benjamin of Tudela was a great traveller in the south of Europe, in Asia, and in Africa. His works have been translated into most European languages.

But the most powerful light of this age was the great Maimonides, the Jewish Aristotle. With him we can hardly deal adequately here.

In the thirteenth century we find Bachiel Ibn Alconstantine, a great physician and favourite of King Jayme.

Among the prominent physicians and men of science of this period, I would mention Abraham of Aragon, and Faragut (Farag Ibn Salomo). The former was the most celebrated oculist of his period; and when the brother of King Louis IX. of France, the Count of Poitou and Toulouse, was stricken with disease of the eyes, they had to beg for help from this skilled man. Faragut was physician to Charles of Anjou, King of Sicily, and was far famed as a man of science. So, also, in the north of Italy, was Hillel of Verona, a philosopher, physician, and writer in Hebrew and Latin. He was a follower of Maimonides.

In France the Jews still maintained a high intellectual standard in the south, but even in the north such men as Rabbi Tam, of Paris, kept the light of their intellectual life burning. Some emigrated from Spain to France, for instance the founder of the Ibn Tibbon family.

In Spain we find a member of the old Abulafia family, Todras Ben Joseph Halevi, prominent at the court of Sancho IV. and his queen, Maria de Molina. In the beginning of the fourteenth century, Jehuda Ibn Waker was powerful at the court of the Regent Don Juan Emanuel; while Samuel Ibn Waker, the astronomer and physician, was high in the favour of Alphonso XI. At the court of this monarch we hear of Don Joseph de Ecija (Benveniste Halevi), who was treasurer to the king and *privado*, or privy-councillor. We are told that he drove in his state-coach surrounded by knights, and that he was splendid in his hospitality.

About this time it seemed as if the intellectual influence of the Jews would become more directly efficacious in the whole of Europe; and, if the religious prejudices on both sides had not made such interaction difficult, the debt of modern civilisation to Judaism would

certainly have been even greater than it now
is. Robert of Anjou, King of Naples, was an
admirer of Jewish culture, and had as his
teacher in Hebrew Leone Romano, who introduced him to Jewish literature; while, at
the same time, Leone turned his attention
to scholastic philosophy, and translated into
Hebrew the writings of Albertus Magnus and
Thomas Aquinas. At the instigation of the
king, Shemarja Ikriti wrote a commentary to
the Old Testament, which he dedicated to the
king. While the king was in the south of
France he made the acquaintance and drew
into his circle the Jewish satirist, Kalonymos
Ben Kalonymos (born 1284 and died 1337).
In his youth this Kalonymos translated philosophical, medical, and astronomical works into
Hebrew from the Arabic. He also wrote ethical treatises. But when, with recommenda-
tions from King Robert, he settled at Rome,
he wrote a satire on the eccentricities of the
Talmud, and this satirical vein runs through
his ethical writings. We feel a breath of the
Renaissance wafted through the Jewish severity of the day. We approach this spirit still
more closely in Emanuel Ben Solomon Romi,
a native of Rome and a friend of Dante. His

was a light and satirical muse, perhaps sometimes too light; he might be compared to Boccaccio rather than to Dante. But the points of similarity to the greatest Italian poet still exist. As Dante comprised all scholastic and classical tendencies of his time within his own personality, so Romi is master of the Biblical, Talmudic, and Neo-Hebraic elements, while the nascent form of Italian poetry (he also wrote Italian poems) greatly influenced his own form of composition. But it is no doubt startling to find the weighty and dignified Hebrew language turned into the lightest forms which satire, the novel, and parody bring with them. As a curious pendant to Dante's *Divine Comedy*, he wrote, as Graetz puts it, a human comedy. He is led through the Inferno by a friend Daniel, where he meets all the wicked of the world, including Aristotle, because he had taught the eternity of the world, and Plato, because he had taught the reality of ideas. And so he wanders through the Inferno and to the gates of Paradise, into which he enters and is graciously received by all the blessed dwellers in this happy abode. The poem is full throughout of satirical allusions, often veiled under a serious form.

M

Towards the close of the thirteenth century Don Meir de Malea was treasurer (*almoxarif*) of Alphonso X., surnamed The Wise, and his son, Don Zag, succeeded him in the office. The court physician of this king was a certain Don Judah Ben Moses Cohen. The king's astronomer, Don Zag Ibn Said, made the astronomical tables which have since been called the Alphonsian Tables. There were other Jewish men of science at the court of Alphonso.

In Castile, in the fourteenth century, another member of the Abulafia-Halevi family, Don Samuel Ben Meir, was the private adviser (*privado*) of King Don Pedro. At the same court there was Abraham Ibn Zarzal, his physician and astrologer. Under Henry II. of Castile, Don Joseph Pichon stood in high favour, as did Don Samuel Abrabanel.

At the court of Aragon, under Don Pedro IV. and Juan I., Chasdai Crescas and Isaac Ben Sheshet held high positions, and were men of great refinement and culture.

In Portugal at this time King Don Ferdinand had two Jews as his immediate advisers, Don Judah and Don David Negro.

The fate of the Jews during the time of the Inquisition was no doubt a very sad one, but their social position was still very high. Nay, this was no doubt the cause of much of the opposition with which they met. The severest wounds were often struck by those who had been renegades from their own camp; as, for instance, by Paul de Santa Maria, or Paulus Burgenses (Solomon Halevi, of Burgos). He tried to convert two prominent Jews of his age without success, both physicians: the one, Joseph Orabuena, physician to Charles III. of Navarra; the other, Meir Alguades, physician to Don Henry III. of Castile. The physician Josua Ben Joseph Lorqui, of Canis, and Chasdai Crescas wrote critical answers to the attacks of Santa Maria.

Owing to forcible conversion during this period, a number of prominent men became Neo-Christians. Among these were Profiat Duran, physician, astronomer, and historian, and David En Bonet Buen Giorn, the former of whom emigrated and returned to his old faith. The physician of Pope Benedict XIII., Josua Lorqui, or Jerome de Santa Fé, was one of these. Juan de Pacheco, a member of the Jewish family Ruy Capon, was, as a Neo-Christian, the chief ruler of Castile under Henry V. To this class also belonged Don Pedro de la

Cabbalaria, who stood close to Queen Isabella. So, too, the minister Diego Arias Davila, whose son Juan was Bishop of Segovia. The conspiracy against the inquisitors at Seville was headed by the Neo-Christians Diego da Sasan and Juan Fuan Abulafia. Such Neo-Christians also were the family of Coronel.

Among the Jews who in this time of persecution remained true to their faith and were still prominent were Don Vidal Ben Veniste Ibn Labi (Ferrer), of Saragossa, the son of Solomon de la Cabbalaria, physician and poet, and highly respected; Joseph Albo, of Monreal; and Abraham Ben Venesti, the friend of King Juan II. Henry IV. of Castile also had as his physician Jacob Ibn Nunes; while Don Juan II. of Aragon was cured of cataract of both eyes by the celebrated oculist Don Abiatar Ibn Crescas Ha Cohen. A most important position with Ferdinand and Isabella was held by Don Abraham Senior, to whom Isabella was so grateful that she gave him a pension for life.

In Italy, in the second half of the fifteenth century, the wealthiest financier of the time was a certain Jechiel of Pisa. But it was chiefly as physicians that they were sought after. Among the most celebrated of these were Guiglielmo de Portaleone, of Mantua, and Messer Leon, of Naples, who was a physician at Mantua, and was learned as a scholar and philologist. The most interesting figure among the Jews in Italy was Elia del Medigo, or Elia Cretensis, who, of German family settled in Crete, had returned to Italy. He wrote in Latin and Greek, and became the teacher of Pico de Mirandola. A quarrel between the learned men of the University of Padua was referred to him for arbitration, and he was made Professor of Philosophy at this university, and lectured here as well as at Florence.

In Germany the Emperor Frederick III. was the friend of the Jews, and recommended them to his son Maximilian on his death-bed. He had as his physician Jacob Ben Jechiel Loans, upon whom he conferred knighthood. The son of Jacob, Goselin Loans, of Rossheim (born 1478, died 1555), was the head of the Jews in Germany during this period, and was called their regent or commander. It was he who taught Reuchlin the elements of Hebrew.

The greatest Jewish family of this period were the Abrabanels, and to this family belonged the last of the Jewish statesmen in

Spain, Don Isaac Abrabanel. He was also a learned man and an author. He was financial adviser to Alphonso v. of Portugal, the friend of the Duke Ferdinand de Braganza, and highly popular with people of all classes and faiths. Being a friend of the Duke of Braganza, he became the victim of the enmity between the king, Joan II., the son of Alphonso v., and the duke ; and thus he left his home and wandered through Spain, where he devoted himself to study. Here Ferdinand and Isabella called him to assist them with his financial experience, which he did with success, and he was rewarded with honours by these monarchs. But his high position and influence could not avert the great misfortune which befell the Jews in Spain, and he himself became a martyr to the cause and left with his brethren. At first he turned to Naples, where he was again invited to stay by Ferdinand 1. and his son Alphonso, whom he followed to Sicily when the French entered Naples. He then fled to Corfu, then to Monopoli in Apulia, and at last died at Venice, where his sons Isaac and Samuel lived, the one a physician, the other a statesman. His eldest son settled at Genoa as physician to Gonsalvo de Cordova, the conqueror

of Naples, where he chiefly devoted himself
to the study of mathematics, philosophy, and
philology.

The youngest son of Isaac Abrabanel was
the most conspicuous Jew in Italy at the close
of the fifteenth and during the first half of
the sixteenth centuries. The wealth which he
acquired enabled him to use it for the benefit
of others, and this generosity of his is referred
to by the Neo-Christian poet Samuel Usque
in the most glowing terms. His wife Benvenista Abrabanella was an equally remarkable woman. She became the companion of
Leonora, the daughter of Don Pedro, Viceroy
of Naples; and when Leonora became Duchess
of Tuscany she retained her warm affection
for Benvenista, whom she called 'mother.'
The Abrabanels' house became a centre for
men of letters and science of all faiths.

It is useless to continue the list of brilliant
men who suffered expulsion or death at the
hands of the Inquisition. But as I have said
before, it must not be supposed that with the
expulsion of the Jews from Spain remarkable
men who held prominent positions ceased to
be found among them.

In spite of all their efforts, seconded by

those of the Neo-Christian Duarte Depaz
(a knight and commander of the Order of
Christ), the Jews were also expelled from
Portugal.

Strange to say, many of them found their
way to Italy, where, as we have seen, there
were already many distinguished Jews. At
Genoa, Joseph Cohen was physician to the
Doge Andrea Doria. He, as well as Solomon
Ibn Verga, and the still more celebrated
Samuel Usque (who, with his brothers Duarte
Gomez and Duarte Pinel, settled at Ferrara),
took upon themselves the task of writing the
history of the Jews. The works of Samuel
Usque are of the very highest quality.   At
Ancona, where for a considerable time the
Jews were very prosperous, Amatus Lusitanus,
the celebrated physician, may be singled out.
The family of Soncin had printing-presses
in Lombardy as well as in Constantinople
and at Prague. In Italy a member of the
old Jewish family Dei Rossi (of whom celebrated descendants, since converted, still exist),
Asarga Ben Mose Dei Rossi, was one of the
most learned men of his time, not only in the
Talmud, but in the Hellenic Jewish writings
of Philo, Josephus, and the Church fathers.

In his works he compared critically the collateral evidence of the Talmud and of classical profane literature. The celebrated doctors in Italy, David de Pomis and Elia Montalto, must also be mentioned. The Latin work of the latter, called *The Hebrew Physician*, is well worth reading. Sixtus v. had as his financial adviser a Neo-Christian named Lopes, who fled from Portugal. I must also notice Leon Modena (born 1571, died 1649), one of the most versatile of men in history, who had many Christian pupils, among them Bishop Jacob Plantavicini and Jacob Gaffarelli. I ought also to mention Joseph Solomon Delmedigo, who was a pupil of Galileo. The family of Luzzato, of Venice and Padua, especially Simon and Moses, were remarkable men ; the one as a writer in prose, the other as a poet who wrote dramas and psalms. Moses Luzzato died 1747.

The fate of several of the prominent Jews who took refuge in Turkey is interesting. The banking-house of Mendes was at the time a European power. The transactions of this firm with the Emperor Charles v. with the King of France, and many other princes, contributed to the sufferings of the family. The

most remarkable figure in this family was
Dona Gracia, a noble woman. From Antwerp
she was driven with her family to Venice,
where they could not remain in safety; then
they fled, and took refuge from the greed of
the monarchs in Turkey, where they were
protected by the Sultan Suleiman. Her final
resting-place was Ferrara. In 1553 she joined
her nephew, Joan Miques, who had married
her daughter Reima, at Constantinople. This
Joan Miques became one of the most remarkable personalities in Jewish history. He was
one of the Marranos, and had to flee from
Portugal. He arrived at Constantinople with
letters of recommendation from the French
diplomats. The sultan soon recognised in
him great political power, and he was made a
Turkish bey. He brought about a reconcilia-
tion between the sultan and his son Selim,
and became his friend and nobleman of his
guard. The sultan gave him land on the lake
Tiberias, in Palestine, in order that he might
reconstruct the ancient city, which was to be
populated exclusively by Jews. When Selim
II. succeeded his father in 1566, Joan was
created Duke of Naxos, and was the most
powerful man in Turkey after the sultan.

Ambassadors and monarchs had to crave for his assistance, and he became one of the great powers in the European politics of the time. He at one time formed the plan of founding a Jewish state at Tiberias, which he rebuilt, and in which he even had the idea of starting factories to compete against Venice. But his plan was not realised. Next to him, the physician Solomon Ashkenazi was the most influential man in Turkey. He was chosen by the sultan as the ambassador to conclude a treaty of peace with Venice, which he signed in the name of the Porte.

As we have seen, the most important band of Spanish and Portuguese exiles settled in Holland, at Amsterdam. Prominent among these was the Consul Pallache, Jacob Tirado, the learned Moses Halevi, the poet Jacob Israel Belmonte, and Alonso de Herrara, a descendant of Gonsalo de Cordova, the conqueror of Naples, who, upon leaving Spain, returned to Judaism in Holland. Another poet was David Jesurun; while de Pina, another Neo-Christian joined Jesurun there and took the name of Rohel Jesurun. The first Jews who were buried in the Jewish cemetery at Amsterdam, founded in 1614, were Emanuel Pimental, a

playfellow of King Henry IV. of France,
called by him King of the Players, and Elia
Felice Montalto, at first Neo-Christian, and
then returning to Judaism. He was a
celebrated physician and author who lived
in Livorno, Venice, and at last at Paris, where
he was physician to Mary of Medici. He
died at Tours, and the queen had his corpse
embalmed and sent to Amsterdam. Further
accretions to the community of Amsterdam
were Isaac de Rocamoro, formerly a monk
under the name of Fray Vicente de Rocamoro.
He was confessor to the Infanta Maria, subsequently Empress of Germany. He joined the
Jewish community of Amsterdam. So, also,
did Enriquez de Paz of Segovia, the Jewish
Calderon. In his youth he was an officer in
the army, and distinguished himself through
his bravery, receiving the order of San Miguel
and being raised to a captaincy. His *nom de
plume* was Antonio Enriquez de Gomez. He
wrote over twenty-two comedies in Spanish,
which were much admired at Madrid. He
had to flee before the Inquisition, lived for
a time in France, and then settled at Amsterdam. Of the wealthy merchant's family Penso,
one member, Felice Joseph, also known under

the name of De la Vega, wrote poems and
Hebrew dramas. There were so many poets
at Amsterdam that an academy of poetry was
started there. There were also students of
science and philosophy, among whom Bal-
thasar Orobio de Castro was perhaps the most
prominent. We may also mention as a man
of great wealth Isaac Suaso, created Baron
Avernes de Gras, who could advance two
million guilders to William of Orange when
he went to England to seek the crown, saying,
'If you succeed, you will repay me; if not I
shall lose it.' Francisco Melo assisted the
state of Holland with his wealth; while a
certain De Pinto left several millions for
charitable purposes, not only to Jewish institutions, but to the state, to Christian
orphanages, and even priests. So, also, the
Texeiras and Daniel Abenser, of Hamburg,
advanced money to the crown of Poland,
while Solomon de Medina, knighted by Queen
Anne, was one of the wealthiest merchants of
London.

Among the members of the community at
Hamburg, the earliest and most prominent
were the family of the Texeiras, of which the
wealthy founder of the bank of Hamburg,

Diego Texeira de Mattos, of Portuguese origin, a nobleman and formerly Spanish minister-resident in Flanders, was the most prominent. When an old man, he returned to his Jewish faith. The brilliant social life they led was to no small degree the cause of their finding some enemies at Hamburg who were jealous of them.

Benjamin Musafia was the physician to King Christian IV. of Denmark. Duarte Nunes de Costa and Jacob Curiel were the diplomatic agents to the court of Portugal, and Ferdinand IV. created the Jewish author, Emanuel Rosales, a count.

An offshoot of the Amsterdam congregation settled in Brazil, where at Pernambuco they were especially numerous. I have already mentioned the names of some of the prominent families residing in England under Charles II. Many of them have become thoroughly anglicised since then, and from them have sprung a large number of prominent men in the present day.

In France, especially at Bordeaux, there were prominent Jews of old families, among them Isaac Pinto, who afterwards settled at Amsterdam. The family Gradis, at Bordeaux,

were great merchants, whose ships sailed to all
quarters of the globe, and they were highly
honoured in their own city. In Paris, in the
eighteenth century, Rodrigues Pereira was a
man of some note, for he invented a language
for the deaf and dumb before the Abbé de
l'Epée. After this period and especially in
our own times, the number of distinguished
Jews of the type of Cremieux and Jules Simon
in all walks of life has been so great, that it
could only be realised by those who take particular pains to inquire into the origin of many
of the prominent Frenchmen.

Yet, in the eighteenth century and in our
own time, I believe that the intellectual and
moral leadership of the Jews was transferred
from Spain to Germany. The beginning of
this leadership is to be attributed to one man—
namely, Moses Mendelssohn. He was not only
the philosopher who thrilled the whole of cultivated Europe with sympathy and admiration, but the Jews have further to thank him
for the tone of refinement he introduced into
Jewish society at Berlin. The family of the
Mendelssohns, Friedlanders, Hitzigs, Herzes,
and many others, formed, as I have said, a real
centre, with *salons* which were certainly among

the foremost of that capital. The *esprit* and conversation of the ladies of this circle (among whom many became prominent in the literary life of Germany of that date), such as Henrietta Herz and Rahel Lewin (von Ense), attracted into this centre men like the Humboldts, Schleiermacher, Frederick von Schlegel, the great Mirabeau, and many others. But the real influence of this Jewish circle is to be found among the young men who formed a league for the purpose of giving vent to their higher intellectual and moral aspirations. They had their literary organ, and it is no doubt that here the first seeds of the poetic productions of Heine were sown, for their influence penetrated throughout the whole of Germany. The poet Boerne, too, is one of the leading lights in the life of the Jews in the first half of this century. Since then, as I have said in the beginning of this chapter, the influence of individual Jews in the establishment of the high intellectual standard which prevails in Germany can hardly be over-estimated. Among the Jews or descendants of Jews, there are so many shining lights in the Germany of to-day that an enumeration of them would be an endless task. But it is not only in their intellectual achievements that they shine in that country. I maintain that some circles of Jews in all the German cities manifest social refinement and culture not to be surpassed by any social groups in the German empire; and whoever has had the good fortune of being introduced into such circles will have to admit that, according to German standards, he can hardly find more thorough specimens of gentlemen and ladies in every sense of those terms.

At the close of these remarks, I cannot help feeling that I have dwelt too much on the brilliancy of the surface life of the Jewish people, and I may appear to attach too much value to the outer glitter of the guinea stamp. For it is, after all, owing to the inner moral and intellectual qualities of the Jewish people that they have a claim to the respect of all right-minded men. But in this chapter I have merely set myself the task, independently of the value of such considerations to serious-minded men, of settling a question of fact, though it be only a surface fact, in the national life of the Jews. I have dealt with the outer appearance independently of that which is within, and it appears to me that in this respect also the claims of the Jews are as high

N

as those of any other group of men which we can distinguish in modern Occidental states, and much higher than those of most. But in their intellectual life their claims must be admitted to be still higher.

IV

THE INFLUENCE OF THE JEWS UPON THE CIVILISATION OF THE MIDDLE AGES

THE facts which are here given concerning the intellectual life of the Jews in the Middle Ages are taken from the work of the late Professor M. J. Schleiden. This man, one of the brilliant lights of German science, was born in the year 1804, of Protestant parents, at Hamburg, where he received most of his schooling. In 1824 he entered the University of Heidelberg as a student of law, and after three years' work at this university, turned his attention to the study of medicine at Göttingen and at Berlin, and finally specialised in the study of botany. In 1839 he was made professor of this subject in the University of Jena, which chair he held for many years, exchanging it in 1863 for the same professorship at the University of Dorpat. He died in 1881, and left behind him one of

the greatest names as a votary of his science,
and a loving remembrance among all those
who knew him as a man of the purest and
noblest character. In 1842-3 he published his
Principles of Botany, in which he was one of
the first to apply the modern inductive method,
and one of the fighters for those principles of
scientific investigation which have now been
adopted, to the benefit and the advancement of
the whole of European thought. Besides his
more popular work, *Plants and their Life*, he
also wrote on the physiology of animals as well
as of plants, and contributed many valuable
and important monographs on that and other
subjects. There is no doubt that his inquiries
into the history of botany first led him to
consider the subject in which we are here
interested. But at the same time the fact of
his taking up this cause gives proof of a
chivalrous nature roused to a healthy indigna-
tion by the wrongs suffered by a weaker
minority; and I believe that it will stand as
a monument in proof of a noble heart, as his
other works will be a lasting record of his intellectual greatness. So admirable is his work
that I cannot do better than translate the most
important portions of it, and I shall indicate

any deviation from his own words in the course of my translation.[1]   He begins thus:

'My work in connection with the history of botany necessarily led me to the writings of Albertus Magnus.   His position with regard to Thomas Aquinas, his dependence upon Aristotle and upon Arabian authors naturally suggested the question as to the relation of these thinkers to one another and to earlier common sources.   I was carried further and further in my investigations, until there came to me a clear insight into a group of facts which our greater historical works entirely ignore, but which have nevertheless been of vital influence in directing the development of civilised humanity.   A short survey of the facts I have thus found is presented in the following essay.

'The Jews are, and remain, the most remarkable of peoples; and if one wishes to adopt the symbolism of a Providential dispensation, one may well call them " the chosen people."   The mere fact that they have not only maintained themselves as a people, true

---

[1] Professor Schleiden's Essay first appeared in Westermann's *Illustrirte Deutsche Monatschrift*, and has been published separately at Leipzig (Baumgartner's), 1877, under the title, ' Die Bedeutung der Juden für Erhaltung und Wiederbelebung der Wissenschaften im Mittelalter.'

to their original spiritual character, for more
than two thousand years—and this in spite of
the dire and bloody persecution which they
have sustained at the hands of the pagan
world, the Persians, the Mohammedans, and
the Christians—but that they are continually
growing and spreading in greater proportion
than any other people, in this and every
climate, ought to present in their life the most
interesting task for a serious and refined study
of history. They are the oldest people standing before the world as the bearer of pure
monotheism, and because of the very purity of
their faith in God they have established and
have clung to the moral law as the real and
true manifestation of religious service. The
whole of Europe has had its Middle Ages, a
period of coarseness, of intellectual and moral
decay, sadder than any imagination can depict;
only the Jews make an exception. In spite
of dispersion and oppression which robbed them
of the simplest rights of man—nay, his very
right to live—the development of their intellectual life has been continuous, and has preserved for the other nations, and has handed
over to them, the foundations of morality and
of spiritual life. But, as is often the case with

natures endowed with moral nobility, they sometimes faltered when fortunate moments made life too easy for them; but every annoyance and every misery which only left them a half-human existence merely had a result to ennoble them, to revive them into renewed exertion towards higher moral and intellectual aims.

'The devastation of Jewish lands by the Assyrians and Babylonians led them in the first place to concentrate themselves as regards their own mental life, and to collect into a unity the total intellectual gain of their previous spiritual life. In the form of the Pentateuch, the Psalms and Prophets, they have presented even the Christian world of our day with a source of devotion and inspiration. Now the Jews carried the blessing they had thus won into their life. Unshakable faith in God and moral conduct, as far as it had already manifested itself to them as duty, gave them the strength of enthusiasm with which this small nation maintained the struggle against the Roman empire for more than a century; so that Rome had to bring more force to bear against them than against any other nation, however great and powerful.

They take their place beside the greatest
heroes whose deeds history records, as well
because of their heroic courage under the
Maccabees, as also during the struggle which
ended with the destruction of Jerusalem under
Titus, the fight of desperation which lasted
for two years under Bar-Kochba, and, later,
their defence of Naples against Belisarius, and
of the Pyrenean passes against the Franks.
They succumbed to the enormous physical
superiority : the nation as such was annihilated,
and the people dispersed over the whole world
from China to India, through Africa and
Europe to the extreme west of the then known
world.   But the people remained a people,
retained an uninterrupted connection among
all its members, and always recognised in the
advancement of its moral and intellectual life
a centre which united them all. Wherever
the Jew went he found people who had community of faith and ideas, and was sure of a
kind reception and of active support.

' There are three factors which stand out as
facilitating the diffusion of intellectual activity
and the fruits of it among the whole of the
Jewish nation.

' First, there was their commercial ability.

The ancients ascribe to the Phœnicians the beginning of commerce. I believe that the geographical term Phœnicians was never sharply defined or meant to be. Phœnicians and Syrians only denoted the Semites who lived more on the coast or more in the interior. Herodotus implies by the term Phœnicians the Syrians carrying on commerce in the Mediterranean. He travelled in Syria about the time of the exile, but does not know an Israel or a Judæa, but only Syrians. His Palestinian Syrians are those who lived more to the south, towards the coast—the Philistines of the Jews; the city he mentions is probably, judging from the route he describes, Gaza. The Israelitish tribes Zebulun, Dan, and Asser carried on commerce by sea and joined the Phœnicians on the sea. That the Israelites were in general bold mariners is proved by their commerce with Ophir under Usia in the eighth century B.C., *i.e.* about the time of the Odyssey, as well as the commercial enterprise of the Jews in the Middle Ages, when the transmaritime commerce was chiefly in their hands. If we consider the bearings of these several facts, we can hardly doubt that among the Phœnicians carrying on maritime commerce there were always Jews who spoke nearly the same language, and were mentally related to them by their former religious education; furthermore, that Jews at once congregated in the colonies founded by the Phœnicians on the north coast of Africa, the Italian islands, at Marseilles, in Spain, etc. They thus readily found connections when, owing to the frequent devastation of their native home, they were led to emigrate. It is thus certain that there existed before our era Jewish communities even at the farthermost point in the west of Europe, while we are already historically assured of their settlement at this time in Assyria, Babylonia, Egypt, and Rome. Paul entered Rome only on his journey to Spain; and he could only have been led to visit Spain because he could count upon the friendly reception of his compatriots there. Taragon, moreover, was called the "Jew City" long before the invasion of the Saracens. These colonies became still more numerous and populous after the destruction of Jerusalem by Titus; and so the whole known world of those days was encompassed by their settlements. Through the many merchants travelling about, they remained in uninterrupted intercourse among each other, and they distributed among their brethren spiritual goods as readily as they did their worldly goods; while the other nations gradually became more and more isolated, and were cut off from the few last sources of spiritual life which were in themselves impoverished. The Romance peoples degenerated, the Germanic races remained for a long time in a state of savagery, and thus the dark Middle Ages grew up, which the Jews never experienced. They, on the contrary, remained in constant communication with the centres of their spiritual life, at whatever place these might for the time have flourished, and they turned thither for counsel and enlightenment whenever they were not able to find the proper decision in some important case.

'The second cause which contributed to the intellectual development of Judaism were these very intellectual centres—namely, the schools which were founded long before our era under Simon Ben Schetach, and were opened to all young men after their sixteenth year (with compulsory attendance) in all larger cities, under Salome Alexendra (79–70), for the study of Scripture and law. There already existed schools of individual famous erudites in Jerusalem and other cities of Judæa, as well as in Egypt at Alexandria. How highly these schools were esteemed by the Jews is shown by the fact that the principal one was called " Kallah," the bride. The best pupil of Hillel, Jochanan Ben Sakkai, in wise anticipation of the future, escaped from the besieged Jerusalem to Vespasian, and gained permission from him to form a school at Jabneh (Jamnia). This was the beginning of a long series of similar institutions, which finally spread over all countries, many of which became famous for science, while several furnished the foundations for Christian academies. In Jabneh the beginning of the elaboration of the Talmud (Mishna and Gemara) was begun.'

Schleiden shows how the Talmud was really the repository for all their science and learning, including law and ethics, and reacting upon their practical life, thus being a mirror of their national and intellectual existence. He then follows up the spread of these Eastern schools, and mentions some of the great men who founded them. In Babylon (where at Pumbadita, for instance, there were twelve

hundred students); Sura, in Arabia, where
the Jews were called 'the people of letters'
(Ahl' ul Kitab). In a footnote he adds that
one could even in our days call them so; and
he quotes from the statistics of Prussia in
1875 with regard to the proportion of those
who could not read or write as follows;

	Males.	Females.
Jews, . . .	3·9 per cent.	5·8 per cent
Protestants, .	6·6 ,,	11·4 ,,
Catholics, . .	15·1 ,,	21·8 ,,

The principal schools often had to change
places, owing to persecution, and Schleiden
adds the following note :—

'It is a noteworthy fact that the Jews were
in all countries only persecuted by morally
base or intellectually degraded princes, but
were protected and advanced by rulers of
superior mental and moral quality. In the
case of the Christians we find the exact contrary down to A.D. 1200.'

After commenting upon the schools of
Tiberias and Jathrib, he maintains that what
is best in the Koran came from the Jews. He
then turns to the rise of Judaism in the West.

'In all larger places of Spain, France, and
Italy there were founded in rapid succession

schools and academies, many of which soon
acquired so great a reputation that they often
attracted Christians and even members of the
clergy who were nearly devoid of opportunities for higher intellectual education. At the
same time there was a rise of Jewish schools
under Arab rule at Bagdad, Kairuan (North
Africa), and Neru (Chorassan). At an early
date there were flourishing schools at Toledo,
Granada, Cordova in Spain; at Lunel, Beziers,
Beaucaire, and Narbonne in France; at Modena, Mantua, Padua, Genoa, Naples, Amalfi,
Benevento, and Rome in Italy, as well as in
innumerable other cities. The foundation of
the medical school of Montpellier was due to
the Jews, and they were also chiefly concerned in the establishment of the Salernitan
school. The rise of the Western schools, which
soon became the equals of those in the East,
and finally eclipsed them, had as a result
the extinction of the last traces of an outer
centralisation of Judaism. From this time on
the Jews were only united by their pure monotheism, their sacred writ, and their moral laws.
The distinction between teacher and people was
almost completely done away with, owing to
the high state of culture to which the people

attained. The teacher was henceforth only a
teacher, and nothing more ; and it is thus that
this period, beginning about the tenth century,
is simply called the Rabbinic period.

'I have only touched upon the main points.
In reality there were innumerable schools of
this kind; for every town of any importance
had one of them, sometimes several. The
number of students who flocked from great
distances to hear some famous teacher was
often above two thousand. And it was not
customary to pay a fee for this teaching; for
the teachers either lived on their own fortune,
or, not unfrequently, on the proceeds of some
definite trade which they followed. It was
a very rare occurrence that a teacher who,
although distinguished, was entirely without
means, allowed himself to be paid by his pupils.
But it happened very frequently that the
teachers partially and even entirely supported
their pupils.

'The third cause which favoured the intellectual growth of the Jews was their linguistic
versatility, for which they appear to have had
a natural predisposition. Even before our era
there were many Jews who spoke Hebrew and
Greek, especially at Alexandria, and to this

Latin was added during the Roman supremacy. Subsequently they learned Syriac, then Arabic; and finally Spanish, French, and German were added to these. In the whole of the Middle Ages there were but few Jews, and those of the lowest class, who did not understand at least two languages; and there are preserved to us names of many men who were thorough masters of from five to seven.

'The religion of the Jews consists simply in the faith in a single Deity, conceived in a purely spiritual manner, and to this was joined the duty to lead a moral life as the essential road to salvation, and as the true form of worship. And as this pure monotheism does not militate against reason or thought, there were no futile quarrels concerning dogmas, and nothing to stand in the way of advancing research. Moreover, their highly developed system of ethics, by which the relation of man to man was ordered, as well as the fact that their feasts, being founded upon historical events, had to be accurately fixed in their cycles, led up to the very gates of science. Their ethics also included the rules of conduct towards the sick and suffering. They were led to philology and critical exegesis by the circumstance that their laws were written in ancient Hebrew, a language not easily understood in later times; the law itself favoured the study of jurisprudence; while the fixing of the dates of festivals encouraged the study of astronomy, and hence of mathematics. Every new development of their actual life, every new condition to which their dispersion forced them to adapt themselves, demanded an enlargement and a development of laws, which were originally meant for definite and simple conditions of life. And, thus stimulated on all sides, they soon came to require the establishment of a logical connection and unity of general principles in all this variety, and were brought to the gate of philosophy as the luminous centre of all intellectual work.

'Another fortunate circumstance must be added to this: as they were free from dogmas, they did not stand in need of a caste of priests. The ceremonies and sacrifices at the Temple of Jerusalem were presided over by priests, but they had no influence upon the faith itself Moreover, the prophets had lowered the value of sacrificial cultus, and with the destruction of the second temple it ceased of itself. Thus the Jews were entirely free from all clerical influence in their intellectual development and in their research. The purity of their faith was protected by the teachers, nay, by the whole people, which would surrender its existence in surrendering its faith in the one God.

'The task of elaborating the whole intellectual history of the Jews since Alexandria is a very attractive one. Such a work, although it would be likely to fill many volumes, is, it appears to me, the more called for, inasmuch as all our historical works completely ignore the Jews the moment they can no longer be struck at with the sword. But I must remain content with a sketch which proves that the spiritual life of the Jews continued in full vitality through the whole of the Middle Ages, and that during the revival of letters and learning their work contributed essentially to the possibility of such a renaissance.'

Schleiden then gives a short sketch of the nature of the Talmud. He refers to the essay of E. Deutsch on this subject, which he considers to give the clearest exposition of its main features.

The Talmud ('study,' from *lamad*, to learn) was verbally collected after Esra, indited in parts for about eight centuries (down to the sixth century), and then written out completely. 'In it are contained all the spiritual aspirations of the Jews in the most diversified directions and towards the most varied objects. It might best be called a chronicle of the civilisation of the Jews during this period.' It is only beginning to have proper treatment and to be made accessible to laymen.

'It is needless to say that in this continuous literary effort for more than two thousand years we meet with vagaries, which are inevitable in the work of man. But as Benjamin Ben Mose said, a thousand years ago, "To carry on research is a duty; to make mistakes is no sin." As early as the eighth century there was opposition to the Talmud. Anan Ben David held up one-sidedly the Old Testament against the Talmud, and created the sect of Karæans as opposed to Rabbinites, who maintained the claims of the Talmud. Such differences occurred in later times, even down to our own days. But physical force, fortunately for them, could never enter into their dispute.

'The bloodless battle for truth was only fought out in the schools, and whoever had her on his side sooner or later proved victorious; and thus what was exaggerated or one-sided was sure to be defeated in the long-run, while the grains of truth inherent even in the exaggeration were assimilated and could act in a fructifying manner.

'In the parts of the Talmud called the Hagada, in which individual rabbis commented upon the serious injunctions and thoughts of the main body of the work in the form of philosophical essays or in poetic episodes, in parables or stories, there are, without doubt, excrescences disfigured by violent imagination and vindictive hatred. But these individual passages are the result of the excitement caused by the cruelties of the time, for which only too often there was abundance of cause. And these portions of the Talmud are only side issues, and in no way render the spirit of the whole.

'It is natural that the intellectual work of the Jewish student was connected in the first instance with the sacred writings of the Old Testament. To understand and to appreciate these fully was the first task.

'Most Christians are inclined to believe that so-called Biblical criticism is their domain and a product of these latter days. If they look back fifteen hundred years they approach nearer to the cradle of this branch of science.

In the middle of the third century Simon Ben Lakish decided that Job had never lived, but that he was the product of a noble poem, and that the names of angels were borrowed by the Jews from a foreign people while they were in exile. Still more important in this direction was the work of Saadia in the ninth century. He placed reason above the Talmud and the Bible, and endeavoured to explain away many miracles in the Bible, *e.g.* the speaking snake in Paradise, Balaam's ass, etc. Saadia translated the Old Testament into Arabic, the most widely-spread language of his time.

'Saadia's contemporary, Chiwi of Balk, applied absolutely rationalistic methods to the criticism of Scripture. In the beginning of the eleventh century Samuel Ben Chofni declared the apparition of the Witch of Endor and the speech of Balaam's ass to be mere hallucinations. Jonah Marinus (also called Abulwalid) worked in the same spirit. He raised Biblical criticism to an independent science. About the same time there lived Ben Jasus (Jizchaki), who proved that the portion of the first book of Moses dealing with the Idumæan kings could not be ascribed to Moses, nay, could not have originated in his

time.   About the middle of the twelfth century
Abraham Ibn Esra published a critical commentary on Isaiah, and even then pointed out
the spurious character of the twenty-third
chapter, which is now universally admitted.

'In the exegesis of the Old Testament the
Jews were no less prominent.   The translation
of Saadia may already be considered as containing exegesis; but even before him a sect
of the Karæans had done important work in
this direction.   Rhabanus Maurus, the learned
Abbot of Fulda, in the eighth century, acknow-
ledges in the preface to his commentary on the
Bible that he has learned much from the Jews
with regard to exegesis.   The Karæan Jews of
Kairo still possess a Bible copied by Rabbi
Aaron Ben Mose Ben Asher, and corrected
according to Masoretan rules.   An excellent
commentary on the Bible and the Talmud, by
Salomon Jizchaki (commonly known as Rashi),
exists in several translations, and has been
used by Christian divines.'

The commentaries to the Talmud are still
more numerous.   From the beginning of the
second century of our era, through the whole
of the Middle Ages down to our time, there is
no century in which some great man has not

produced some work on this subject. I omit Schleiden's account of the prominent workers in this field.

'As has been said, the Jews appear to have an innate talent for languages. No doubt their dispersion among so many different nationalities contributed to this. But the moral earnestness with which they clung to their ethical and religious convictions was the most important factor, leading them to exert their diligence and ingenuity in the study of the Oriental languages in which the fundamental principles of their moral and religious life are imbedded. If this had not been so, we of modern times might have stood before the Hebrew language as much puzzled as we have been in approaching hieroglyphics. It is true that Origenes, and after him, especially, Jerome, studied Hebrew with rabbis in order to understand the Old Testament; but with these all deeper and more serious study of Hebrew ceases among the Christian clergy. They remained content with the miserable Latin translation, and they could often not read this with complete understanding.

'The foundations of the deeper study of language which we call linguistics were laid by

the Jews nearly twelve hundred years ago.
Juda Ben Koreish proved as early as the time
of Saadia that Hebrew, Arabic, and Chaldean
were all three branches of the same linguistic
root, the same in all essential features. The
etymological Hebrew dictionary of Menahem
Ben Saruc was completed and corrected in
many points by Dunash Ben Labrat. Juda
Chajug (Abu Sakaria Jachia) recognised the
principle of the three letters for all Hebrew
roots. The original Hebrew script was want-
ing in all signs for definite vowels. It was
thus difficult to read, and the people were
beginning to become estranged from it. After
A.D. 550, learned men in Assyria invented a
system of vowel symbols, and this system was
developed in the seventh century by Mocha
and his son Moses, and was called the younger
Tiberiensian system, which is now in general
use. The text of the Bible written according to
these principles by Moses and Aaron Ben Asher
have formed the basis for all subsequent study
of the Hebrew text of the Old Testament.

'In the eleventh century, Marinus (Abulwalid Ibn Ganach) wrote a complete Hebrew
grammar and dictionary which formed a basis
for all subsequent study, and are still of great

value. He was the first who raised exegesis to the rank of a true science. After him Nathan Ben Jechiel wrote a dictionary to the Talmud, which is used even now. The Jews in those days wrote their books in Arabic as frequently as they did in Hebrew, but those who lived in Christian countries always translated the Arabic works into Hebrew. Samuel Halevi Ibn Nagrela (993-1055) knew Hebrew, Chaldean, Arabic, Barb, Castilian, and Latin. As early as the time of the Visigoths the Jews wrote treatises against Christianity in clever Latin, and they were justified in their contempt of the coarse and ignorant Christians who lived under the Moors (Muzarabs), who learned Arabic but soon forgot their Latin, and with it their whole religion. In the thirteenth century the famous Levi Ben Gerson (Ralbag) wrote a book called *The Battles of the Lord*, in which there occurs a very ingenious disquisition on the origin of language. Moses Ben Esra spoke Hebrew, Arabic, Persian, Greek, and Spanish. To cut short this catalogue of Jewish philologists, I would close it by mentioning the families of the Kimchi, Tibbon, and Kalonymos, who for several generations were famous as philologists and translators. We still possess a very valuable work containing a grammar and a lexicon of David Kimchi, and another grammar by Moses Kimchi.

'If one studies the history of the Reformation and realises how absolutely necessary it was to recall into life a thorough knowledge of the whole Bible in the original text, one will be forced to say: "Without Hebrew no Reformation, and without Jews no Hebrew; for they were the only teachers of this language."'

Schleiden also casts a rapid glance at the Jewish Hellenic literature of Alexandria. He points to the writings of Aristeas, of Philo, to the elaboration of the third book of the Maccabees, and the book of Wisdom about the first half of the first century A.D.; and, before this, the Jewish Sibyl, Pseudo-Phokylides, the book of Esther, Bel and the Dragon of Babel, as well as the letters of Jeremiah. Quite recently numerous and important additions have been made to this literature in the discovery of manuscripts belonging to this period.

Schleiden then turns his attention to the influence which these early schools had upon the study of philosophy. 'In the second century Rabbi Meïr is occupied with philosophical

work, and is in close intercourse with the
Neoplatonic philosopher Numenios. As early
as the third century A.D., Rabbi Simlai made
the first attempt to treat the Agada philosophically. In the ninth century, Saadia Ben
Joseph, chief of the school of Sura, began an
attempt to give a philosophical foundation to
the religion of the Jews. In his systematic
work, *Belief and Dogma (Emunot we Deot)*, he
considers reason to be the judge of Scripture
and the Talmud, and holds Judaism to be
only a confirmation of rationalism revealed
by God in order to shorten the road to truth
for those less gifted. He was opposed to the
teleological view because the human conception
of purpose could not be applied to God. He
demanded that the words of Scripture should
always be construed in their natural sense, in
so far as they do not contradict perceptible
facts or reason, and in so far as they do not
contradict one another. The learned Arabs
held his work in high esteem, and his principles are still mentioned by Jewish students
in our day.

'Among the last teachers of the school of
Pumbadita, Rabbi Hai is distinguished. He
was a decided opponent of all mysticism and

superstition, all craving for miracles and magic. All this he considered pure invention and deception, and, if attempted in the name of God, sacrilege. With his free spirit he often took counsel concerning certain passages in Scripture with the learned Mar Elia I., the wise Catholicus of the Eastern Christians of Bagdad. When some rabbis reproached him with this, he answered: " According to the Talmud a Jew is bound to accept truth from everybody."

'In the eleventh century the philosophical works of the poets Gabirol and Yehuda Ben Halevi were also of interest; the former was, even in his youth, acquainted with Socrates, Plato, Aristotle, the Neoplatonic and Arabian philosophers. Led by these he became the first independent thinker in Europe, since Justinian's brutality had caused the philosophical schools of Athens to be closed, and Scotus Erigena (850) was as good as forgotten. His chief work was *Mekor Chajim* (*The Source of Life*). It was written in Arabic, was then translated into Latin by a Christian priest under the wrong name of *Avicebron*, and in later times translated into Hebrew by a Jew. Many were indebted to this book for

the wisdom which they extracted from it,
so William of Auvergne, Albertus Magnus,
Thomas Aquinas, and Duns Scotus.'

'The acme of the philosophical development
is reached in the twelfth century.'   At this
point Schleiden mentions the Sohar, and maintains that the common view of the Kabbala is
a mistaken one, inasmuch as only its degenerate portions have been considered.   'The aim
of the mediæval Christian Church, especially of
scholastic philosophy, was a hopeless struggle
to realise the dream of the "God-man":
to amalgamate, nay, to identify, the pure
spiritualism of religious Hebraism, with the
pure sensuousness of religious Hellenism.   The
contagion of this tendency also reached Judaism in that school which endeavoured to grasp
the sensuous language of the prophets in
their literary significance, and so anthropomor-
phise God.   This took place in the Kabbala.
The Sohar, belonging to this class, and forming
its chief work, gives quite a different idea
from the one generally current.'   Schleiden
refers to Frank's work, *La Kabbale*, as giving
a just view.   'The unity and immaterial
character of God, the immortality of the
soul, and freedom of the will, control the

whole of this work and give it a higher significance.'

'In the same century Joseph Ibn Zadic wrote a system of logic. Abraham Ibn Daud also published about this time his work entitled *The Highest Faith*, the burden of which may be summarised in the following sentence: "The ultimate purpose of all philosophical theory is the practical realisation of moral aims, and in this consists Judaism." No philosophy has ever expressed a higher aim. It is exactly the same as what the philosopher Fries put seven hundred years later into the technical words, "The Primate of Practical Reason."

'May this suffice, though a hundred names of other philosophers must be omitted. I would now turn to one man, the greatest whom the whole of Europe can show in this century—namely, Maimonides. Ibn Amran Musa Ben Abdallah, or Moses Ben Maimun (1135-1204), is only known imperfectly, as his life-history is full of legends. But so much we do know, that in his whole life he was penetrated with the purest morality and by the highest nobility of soul. His father, a man of high position in Cordova, was a mathematician, astronomer, and Talmudic student, and

inspired his son with an enthusiasm for science
at an early date.   Driven out of their home
by the Al-mohads, the family led for a long
time a homeless life.   Maimonides learned
from his father all that he could teach him,
while Mohammedan teachers introduced him
into the natural sciences and the study of
medicine.   The view that he was a pupil of
Averroes has long since been shown to be
erroneous.   Maimonides stood completely on
the ground of Judaism as well as on that of
the Greeks.   If anything he was a follower
of Aristotle, though quite independent and
often differing from him.   He also studied
Socrates, Xenophon, and Plato; furthermore,
the Stoics, the peripatetic Alexander of Aph-
rodisias, and the eclectic Themistius.   Of
course, he was limited by the age in which he
lived, his surroundings, and the oppression to
which the Jews at that time were subjected.
He cannot be reproached with this, as no one
can emancipate himself from such influence;
but he stands high above many rabbis when
he says, "They find in the Holy Scripture a
hundred things of which Scripture has never
dreamt."   His great philosophical work is
called *Morch ha-Nebuchim* (*Guide of the Err-*

ing). He himself says concerning it: " In short, I am thus made, that if a thought fills me, and I can only express it in such a form that it satisfies and advances but one thoughtful man among ten thousand, while it may prove unbearable to the great mass of the people, I will pronounce boldly and openly a word that brings light to the reasonable, though the blame of the unreasonable crowd be heaped upon me." And he has enlightened the thoughtful and has exerted a powerful influence upon the development of philosophy. Scaliger says : " The *Guide of the Erring* can never be praised sufficiently." Casaubonus says of it : " What belongs to religion he treats religiously, the philosophical philosophically, and the divine divinely." This is the estimate which the age following his own placed upon him. The motto, as it were, of his work was : " Man is not to be led in his actions by mere authority. Never turn your back upon your better knowledge ; for have we not our eyes in front, and not behind ? " In another passage he says : " The aim of religion is to learn to think and to act in harmony with reason, in order to approach to perfection." In both respects he stands high above

Christian scholastic philosophy, which moreover rests upon his foundations.   His work
was translated many times into Latin, German,
Spanish, English, etc.   Joel has shown how dependent even Spinoza was upon Maimonides.

'I must select two philosophers from the
period succeeding Maimonides.   First, Levi
Ben Gerson, who is an ardent admirer and
a warm defender of the philosophy of Maimonides, and must be looked upon as his
successor.   His work, *Milchamoth*, attracted
great attention, not only among the Jews, but
among men like Pico of Mirandola, Reuchlin,
and Kepler.   The other is Chasdai Crescas,
who in many ways was a just opponent of
Maimonides; but is especially remarkable because he was the first to combat systematically
the philosophy of Aristotle and to subject
Aristotle's metaphysical and physical views to
a careful critical examination.   He did this
in his book *Or Adonai* (*The Light of God*),
which appeared in 1410, long before Christian
students dared to oppose the prevailing Aristotelian views.   Thus with regard to philosophy, one might also say : Without Judaism
no scholastics and no advance, and therefore
no development in philosophy.

P

'Before closing this survey of their philosophical work, I must mention Isaac Ben Moses Halevy (Prophiat Duran), who subjected Christian dogmas to close criticism in a series of letters addressed to a converted Jew.

'I now turn to a special branch of philosophy (ethics), which held a high position in Judaism, if only because of the fact that, since the destruction of their church-services in Jerusalem, there only remained to them this form of serving God, which they had already practised from the earliest time.

'I must first draw attention to one point which unites ethics to the philosophy of religion—namely, tolerance. Genuine tolerance is the realisation of one's own nobility of soul, which leads one to treat one's fellow-man always and everywhere, without regard to differing beliefs, humanely and with kindness. It is sufficiently well known that in this respect Christians did not show themselves worthy of praise down to our own days; and this at once does away with the assertion that the commandment of universal charity is peculiar to Christianity. With the Jews we find the exact contrary. They never had the greed of proselytising, and made conversion into their

own faith as difficult as possible. Nay, a
learned rabbi went so far as to express "doubt
of every proselyte even down to the tenth generation." Rabbi Nachmani, who lived in the
fourth century, had the motto, "Live at peace
with thy brothers and relations, with all the
world, even with the heathens." And since
his time the Jews recognise no difference between the orthodox and the heterodox, and
only the rabbis of a few schools appeared to
assert their orthodoxy—*e.g.*, against Maimonides, through a ban which has long since become powerless. The Jews, far from avoid-
ing intercourse with heathens and Christians,
had social communion with them; as, for instance, in common meals, until all this was
forbidden by Christian priests. In the tenth
century an anonymous work appeared in
which kindness, gentleness, and justice against
those of other beliefs are taught, with the
severest threats against those who sin against
such principles. At the very time when in
Spain, France, and Germany the most ini-
quitous persecution raged against the Jews, a
French Jew, Yehuda Sir Leon Ben Isaac (Ha
Chasid, the "pious one"), wrote a guide to
higher religious life, in which he says: "Thou

shalt act righteously always towards the Christians as well as towards those of thine own faith. If they have made a mistake to their own disadvantage, one must point it out to them. If a Jew is collector of taxes, he is not to exact more from the Christian than from the Jew. The Jew is not to use an untrue pretext against the Christian, and he is not even to say to an unsafe borrower that he has no money. One is to take nothing from the Christians, for God helps those who are oppressed," etc. I should think this would already be enough to make ridiculous the mass of prejudice against the Jews.' Schleiden here quotes as a footnote the principle publicly expressed by the Christian Church of those days: " One need not keep one's word to a heretic."

'If we enter more directly into their ethics, I would first say that obedience to the moral law was the foremost and almost the only duty towards God, the religious service proper; and if we leave aside the changing opinions of individuals, the principle of the moral law for the Jew is the striving for perfection which must be satisfied—surely the purest and most unselfish motive. As morality was a religious duty to the Jew, there can exist among them no teacher who does not touch upon questions of ethics and treat of them more or less thoroughly; I will therefore remain content with selecting a few distinguished names whose bearers exerted a wide and enduring influence upon Judaism.

'First, and before all, we must here again mention Hillel and Shammai, whose morality and life stand blameless. Shammai is distinguished from his famous contemporary only in that he more scrupulously founded individual precepts upon the fixed law. No doubt Hillel is more important for us; for his whole teaching was the school of moral purity and of love in which the best of Jesus Christ's teaching is already contained. At this early date the apocryphal Book of Wisdom must also be mentioned which was indited in Alexandria in the time of Caligula, and which has erroneously been ascribed to Philo. It is an attack upon the immorality and idolatry of the pagans. The Jew known under the name of " Pseudo-Phokylides " pursues the same aim and recommends the pure morality of the Jews to the Greeks. I must also mention the patriarch Rabbi Simon, of the second century, whose saying has come down to us:

"The world rests upon three conditions—truth, righteousness, and peace." Rabbi Mar Samuel had great influence in the third century. The prophet Jeremiah had already enjoined upon the exiled Jews: "Further the welfare of the state to which ye have been driven in exile." Samuel raised this to a precept, which was to be universally binding for the Jew, that wherever he might be, the laws of the land should be as binding as are his own. This precept has been accepted by the Jews wherever they have been, and they have lived up to it.

'I omit a long period, and turn to Rabbi Gershom Ben Yehuda, who had a very beneficent influence upon Judaism. In spirit Judaism always favoured monogamy; but it had not expressly forbidden polygamy. This was first done by Gershom. Since that time monogamy remains inviolate. The numerous poems which bear testimony to the beautiful relation between man and wife are most impressive. A special class of these were the bridal songs in which Yehuda Ben Halevi distinguished himself, and which praise the high dignity and sanctity of matrimony. In the eleventh century follows Rabbi Hai, and he expressed his own noble morality in a didactic poem called "Mussar Haskel," which was translated into Latin, and was frequently edited. In the same century there lived Bachia Ben Joseph Ibn Bakuda, the central aim of whose life was expressed in his book *Choboth ha-Lebaboth* (that is, *Duties of the Heart*), in which he advocated the intensifying of the Jewish law with the repression of the ritual laws. He was a "pietist" in the best sense of the word, and strongly leaned towards asceticism. In the following century Yehuda Sir Leon Ben Isaac opposed himself to the ascetic tendency of Rabbi Bachia. He stigmatised as wicked all isolation from human intercourse, and held all forms of monastic life to be immoral. Concerning prayer, he has beautifully said that "it only is of value in the mother-tongue, for in a foreign tongue it leaves the heart empty." Finally, I must also mention in this period Maimonides himself; as in several chapters of his commentary to the Mishna, as well as in his *Moreh ha-Nebuchim*, he has systematised philosophically (chiefly according to Aristotle) the ethics of the Jews, and inasmuch as he frequently refers to this subject in his other works.

'From ethics I am naturally led to law and

jurisprudence, inasmuch as with the Jews the
duties of morality and the duties of law are
hardly distinguished.   A few additions to
what has just been said may therefore suffice.
I have already mentioned Rabbi Simon and
Rabbi Samuel.   Rabbi Hai wrote a book
in Arabic on the commercial law of the
Talmud, which was subsequently translated
into Hebrew.   In the twelfth century Rabbi
Isaac Halevi was distinguished as a teacher of
civil law.   It was universally recognised in the
south of France that the Jewish laws were
better than the Christian ones, a view which
was never refuted, but which was only
condemned as heresy.   The most important
domain in which the Jews effected an essential
change in the limitations of Roman law was
their invention of drafts and letters of credit,
through which also the whole of commerce
experienced a greater extension.   Thus, when
under Philip II., plunder and incendiarism was
renewed in the most shameful manner against
the Jews, the institution of drafts gave them
a possibility to save from the Christian high-
way robbers at least a part of their possessions.

‘The Jews, furthermore, considered hygiene
to be a moral duty; to care for the preserva-

tion of the normal condition of one's body
through proper diet, as well as the care and
restoration to health of those who are diseased.
We therefore find most of their teachers also
educated in medicine, and often members of
the medical profession. How conscientious
they were in the performance of this duty,
can be best realised in the beautiful prayer
which Maimonides wrote for the doctor who
is about to visit a patient. One may say that
until the medical schools at Montpellier and
Salerno (which were chiefly founded by Jews)
were organised, the Jews were almost the
only physicians in the whole of the then
known world. Later the Arabs joined them
in this work, and when these were expelled
from Spain the Jews were again the only
representatives of medical science in Europe.
The brutal and ignorant Christians of that
time even arrived at the absurd superstition
that only the Jews were possessed of the talent
for medicine. Secular and spiritual princes,
who plundered and persecuted the Jews in
the most shameful manner, still refused to
accept a Christian, nay, even a converted
Jew, as their court physician. So Francis I.
of France. There was a time in which the

Jews as court physicians held the lives of all the princes and prelates in their hands. Even in the sixteenth century by far the greater number of the most celebrated physicians were Jews. It will suffice here to mention only a few of the most celebrated physicians, as the importance of the Jews in this profession is beyond all denial. As early as the third century we come upon Rabbi Mar Samuel, whom we have already mentioned. He even then ascribed most diseases to vitiated air, and attributed the greater mortality of those wounded in battles to the longer influence of the air upon their wounds. Farragut [1] was celebrated as a translator and a court physician to Charlemagne. Towards the close of the ninth century Isaac Ben Suleiman Israeli wrote, besides other books, an Arabic work on fevers, which was soon translated into Latin, Spanish, and Hebrew. About the same time, under the Caliph Almamun, Rabbi Mashalla and Rabbi Abul Barkat stood in high repute as physicians in the East. In the thirteenth century Abraham Cabrit wrote a

---

[1] It might be a matter of some pride to the descendants of the American naval hero of this name, if they could establish their descent from this great Hebrew.

commentary to Hippokrates. A far-famed
teacher at Montpellier, about 1300, was Rabbi
Profatius. I must also mention that Maimonides edited Galenus, wrote aphorisms on
medicine, and that he was invited to be court
physician to Richard Cœur de Lion, but
refused the invitation.

'Until the close of the seventeenth century
medicine and natural sciences were not separated from one another. Mathematics and
astronomy were the first to sever this connection. Therefore, all the physicians were also
students of the natural sciences, and it will
hardly be necessary to mention any of these,
especially in this connection. I will limit myself
to mentioning a few explorers. So Petachiah of
Ratisbon, Eldad (Danit), whose travels were
translated into Latin, and, above all, Benjamin
of Tudela, who travelled from 1165 to 1173.
He explored nearly the whole known world of
that day. His book, *Mascot Benjamin* (*Iter
Benjaminum*), has not only been frequently
translated into Latin, but also into nearly every
European language. The Jews also took part
in the discovery of the East Indies, especially
through Abraham de Behia and Joseph Zapa-
tero de Lamego, who were sent by Juan II. to

explore the coast of the Red Sea and the island of Ormuz.[1]

'I now come to the exposition of their merits with regard to astronomy. At an early date the Jews had their own chronology and their own calendar. In order to keep this well regulated, and to define accurately the periods of their festivals, they were obliged to study astronomy; and, as is shown by many passages in the Talmud, and later by Maimonides, the knowledge of the heavenly constellations was recognised as a living stimulus towards the knowledge of God and to piety.

'Already among the successors of Hillel, Gamaliel is praised as a mathematician and astronomer. He is stated even to have used the telescope (of course without glasses) in the year A.D. 89. Jehoshua already knew the seventy (seventy-three) years' cycle of a small comet (Halley's comet). Mar Samuel gave, in a " Boaita," theories on the construction of the heavens; on the sun, moon, stars; on the causes and changes of the seasons, etc. He wrote a special work on the seasons, the manuscript of which still exists in the Vatican. He

[1] Modern research also promises to show that they were concerned in the discovery of America.

was at the same time a decided opponent of astrology, which he despised.

'For a long time the calendar was tied to numerous ancient formalities, and was kept secret by the Sanhedrim, until the patriarch Hillel II. made it public. It corresponds so completely to the Metonian cycle that it has proved useful down to our day. It can hardly now be computed how much of this computation is to be ascribed to Hillel. Before Mohammed, the Arabs received this calendar from the Jewish school at Jathrib. About the year 800, Rabbi Sahal al Tabari (called Rabban) gained a great name as mathematician and astronomer. He was the first to translate Ptolemæus into Arabic, and discovered the refraction of light. Rabbi Abusahal Dunash Ben Tammin, famous as a physician and as an astronomer, was one of the first who used the Arabic numbers which were then introduced. The astronomical works of Rabbi Abraham Ben Chija (*Abargeloni*) about this time were translated into Latin and extensively used. We also possess a thorough and extensive refutation of the astrological superstition by Maimonides, which, however, failed to make Christian priests and princes the wiser. A

very great mathematician of the twelfth
century was John of Savilla or de Luna. He
wrote a practical arithmetic in which, for the
first time, we meet with ciphering with
decimal fractions, probably his own invention. In the thirteenth century I need
only dwell upon the book Sohar, which book
teaches the revolution of the earth about its
axis as the cause of night and day long before
Copernicus. In the middle of the thirteenth
century, Alphonse X., called "the wise," was
raised to the throne of Castile. He manifested
a passion for astronomy, and had new astronomical tables made, which were long used by
astronomers as the "Alphonsian tables." He
intrusted the direction of this enterprise to
the Jewish astronomer Rabbi Isaac Ben Sid.
About the same time Rabbi Judas Ben
Hakohen translated for the same monarch the
astronomical works of Avicenna into Spanish.
To him is also ascribed the division of all the
stars into the forty-eight star pictures. Under
Alphonso XI., Rabbi David Audrahan, Isaac
Ben Samuel, Ben Israel, and Jacob Ben
Tibbon are praised for working out astronomical tables; while Profatius, one of the most
celebrated teachers of medicine at the Academy

of Montpellier, is also distinguished as an astronomer. I must especially mention here again Levi Ben Gershon (Ralbag), better known under the name of Magister Leo de Bagnolas, who had a great reputation as an astronomer. His description of an astronomical instrument which he discovered was translated into Latin at the special request of Pope Clement VI., and Kepler took great pains to procure it.

'All this will suffice to show that up to the thirteenth century the Jews were infinitely superior to their Christian contemporaries in matters intellectual as well as in all the sciences which are of importance to our life. The practical result of this manifests itself in that this superiority was also recognised by their contemporaries. For, as physicians they were not only masters of the life of all the spiritual and secular dignitaries, but they also administered with great frequency the states to which they belonged, be it through their influence, or through the actual state offices which were intrusted to them. Their moral integrity, their intellectual acumen, and their wide experience very often led them to the head of public business among heathens,

Mohammedans, and Christians.   Already
under the Ptolemies the heads of Egyptian
Jewish schools, Onias and Dositheus, had
great influence at court.   Philo was sent by
his community as an ambassador to Rome.
Under the first Roman emperor the Jews were
generally esteemed and had great influence, as
so many laws enacted in their favour show.
So Rabbi Jehoshua stood in high esteem with
Hadrian, and Rabbi Abbahu with Diocletian.
The 144 Novelle of the Codex proved that
the Jews were also esteemed as agriculturists
under Justinian.   The chiefs of the Jewish
academy of Babylon were at the same time
always of political importance, especially under
the better Persian rulers.   They also had
great influence among the Moors, until
Mohammed began to persecute them, after
he considered himself sufficiently strong to
do without them.   Two Jews, Abdallah Ibn
Salam, and Mukchairik, were especially help-
ful to him in the editing of the Koran.'

Schleiden then covers the ground to which
the preceding chapter has been devoted, and
also dwells upon the theoretical work on
statesmanship and history which several of
these great men have left behind them.   He

also gives a survey of the great Jewish poets of the Middle Ages as manifesting their high artistic sense, which was only limited in the scope of its manifestation by the Mosaic interdict of making images. He continues: 'I do not know that the Jew has ever complained of learned and celebrated women as our Schiller has done. If so, he would have found abundance of material in the history of the Jews. So, for instance, in the age of the Tanaim a woman named Berurja was far-famed for her learning. In the twelfth century a beautiful Jewess gave lectures in the East on the Talmud, and Rebecca, the daughter of Rabbi Meïr, the granddaughter of the famous Rashi, wrote several scientific works.

'Inasmuch as the beautiful wedding songs were sung, and as at an early date music was introduced into the service of the synagogue, the Jews must have preserved their familiarity with music which is so often mentioned in the Old Testament. In the eleventh century Jacob Ben Jakar is mentioned as a writer on music; and in the fifteenth century Arkevolte wrote an interesting book on this subject, which, as regards the views therein contained, strongly reminds us of Thiebaut's *Reinheit der Tonkunst*.

'I have until now endeavoured to prove how actively the Jews were striving forward in the path of intellectual advancement, and were developing every side of scientific life through the whole of the Middle Ages, at a time when all European nations were at a stand-still or in retrogression, or—as in the case of the Germanic peoples—hardly made one step in advance; and I have tried to show how much of their spiritual gain accrued to the various European nations who were just beginning a new spiritual life at the close of the Middle Ages. But they have another merit of inestimable magnitude. When the Occidental peoples began longingly to stretch out their hands for the golden fruit of ancient culture, the Jews had to step in and make them accessible to them; for the Christians, in their dense ignorance, did not understand the languages in which the spirit of the ancient world was embodied. If the Jews had not worked as translators, we might have remained fast in the dark Middle Ages for a much longer time. The first people who, after the night of migration of the races with their coarse orgies, developed a new intellectual life were the Arabian Moors, and to them only the Jews opened out the works of ancient Greece.

'Even in the translation of the Old Testament into Greek (the so-called Septuagint) the Jew Aristobulos was especially active; and the book of Jesus Sirach was translated into Greek by his grandson of the same name. In the second century the Greek translation of the Thora by Akylas was made: and in the fourth century the Chaldean (the so-called Targum Onkelos), and before this the Assyrian (the so-called Peshito), were added to it. In the middle of the seventh century Messer Gawaich translated the medical book of Aaron from the Assyrian into Arabic. In the ninth century Rabban (Sahal al Tabari) translated Ptolemæus into Arabic, and Saadia Ben Joseph transferred the Old Testament into the same language. Towards the close of the tenth century Rabbi Joseph Ibn Abitur completed his great work, the Arabian translation of the Mishna, at the request of the caliph Alhakem II. Through the famous Chasdai, Dioskorides first came to Spain as a gift of Constantine VIII. of Byzantium, and was translated through Latin into Arabic with the help of a Greek monk. From this time on works of this class are so frequent that it is hardly worth our while to enumerate names. Whole families took part in such work for several generations; so the Tibbon family, through whom especially the works of Averroes and Aristotle were translated into Latin, and were made accessible to Western Europe. Moses Ibn Tibbon gave an excellent translation of Euclid. The family Kalonymos holds an equally high position in this respect. The Emperor Frederick II. especially valued their services as translators, as well as those of Jacob Anatoli. Finally, we must also mention in this connection the work of the French family Kimchi.

'Casting one more glance back we find that the Jews, through the whole of the dark, mentally sterile, and rotten Middle Ages, were the preservers of a rational agriculture, as of all greater industries, silk culture, dyeing and weaving, and the representatives and advancers of wider commerce—the foundation to the wealth of nations. We have seen that in continuous intellectual exertion they culti-vated the whole region of science, which they advanced until, at the close of the Middle Ages, they could hand it over to the nations

who were about to awaken from their sleep.
They are the founders of scientific philology.
They were the only people who, in contrast to
the narrowness and ignorance of the Christian
clergy, preserved and advanced a thorough
and fruitful knowledge of Scripture; because
for many centuries they alone were familiar
with the Oriental languages, and to a certain
extent even with ancient Greek, together with
the knowledge of the Western tongues.   They
were the only people in whom a development
of intellectual life and philosophy, and
especially philosophy of religion, could find
scope, and who built up a system of morals
such as no other people has done.   It is to
them especially that we owe the scientific
elaboration and advancement of medicine;
they took a most active part in the progress
of astronomy; they founded the famous schools
of Montpellier and Salerno, and contributed
essentially to the flourishing advance of Padua.
But a few years after the invention of the
printing-press they already had excellent
printing establishments in many cities.

'It is with justice that Ribeyra de Santos
says: "We owe to the Jews, more than to
anybody, our first knowledge of philosophy, of

botany, of medicine, of astronomy, of cosmo-
graphy, as well as the elements of grammar
and of the sacred languages, as well as nearly
all studies of biblical literature." '

With this Schleiden closes his treatise, referring the more curious to the numerous
original sources which he has cited.   We cannot help feeling that the scientific integrity of
the man, his extensive studies, and the sources
which he quotes, are a guarantee of the correct-
ness both of his judgment and of the estimate
which he forms of the part which the Jews
have taken in presenting to us who live now
that fruit of culture and civilisation which we
prize as our highest good.

V

I THINK it likely that the foregoing chapter will have been a revelation even to many thoughtful and well-read people. The Jewish nation and its literature are to most people of purely religious interest. Their literature and language, if they are not thus regarded in their religious bearing, are considered a matter of remote antiquity, not directly connected with European life and thought, perhaps even opposed to it. As such matters of antiquarian interest, they are considered on a level with the monuments and language of ancient Egypt, Assyria, and Babylon. But the mediæval and modern aspect of Jewish civilisation, and the fact that it is an essential part of such European history, have been quite ignored, if they are not absolutely unknown.

It makes those who are imbued with the

historical and scientific sense shudder that so
vast and integral a portion of the civilisation
of mediæval Europe should have remained unknown to us. We must realise how imperfect,
nay, how fragmentary, the picture of mediæval
history, as it has been handed down to us, is.
Even now our best efforts to remedy this evil
must be frustrated; and this is owing chiefly
to the neglect and the involuntary one-sidedness of the modern Jewish historians themselves. We have not at hand a work which
will give us an adequate picture of the life,
actual and not only religious, the civilisation
and thought, not only moral and intellectual
but also æsthetic, of the Jewish people in
more modern times. The historical works of
Graetz, Geiger, and others do not adequately
respond to this historical need. There is in
them all an undue preponderance of the religious and martyrological element. And though
this can well be accounted for in the essential
nature of the Jewish people, and of their fate
and history, the result is none the less unsatis-
factory and deplorable. Religion has no doubt
been the central feature of the daily, as well
as of the higher intellectual, life of the Jewish
people, and is thus organically interwoven with

their history; and so, too, have their sufferings and their martyrdom become an almost essential attribute of them as a people. But in their history there are other elements of a brighter nature, which may be suppressed or robbed of their central importance and vitality if these two elements of religion and suffering are magnified out of proportion in an account of their past life. In one word, we desire to have some adequate and truthful record of the life of the Jews since the destruction of the Temple of Jerusalem, at moments when they are neither praying nor suffering—we require what the Germans call a ' Kultur Geschichte ' of the Jews. Where is the learned Jew who will write such a ' Kultur Geschichte ' ? It will, no doubt, be a difficult task, and one which will require in him not only the means of exposition essential to a great historian, but also an absolute familiarity with the Hebrew and other languages, and an intimate acquaintance with the original sources of its vast literature. And where is the great historian of the Middle Ages who will embody this element of mediæval life in his general history, and will thereby supplement our knowledge of that which now remains fragmentary and inaccurate ?

The general student of history may even find that he has neglected a mass of evidence, of historical sources, bearing upon European history independently of its relation to the Jews, scattered throughout their mediæval documents, which may serve as the most important collateral proof with regard to events of European history that rest upon slender foundations of evidence. Not to mention the casual data contained in their general religious literature and in the earliest chronicles, he may find it of the greatest importance to consult the professedly historical works of the three Ibn Vergas and Prophiat Duran in the sixteenth century; the valuable records of Joseph Hakohen concerning the chronicles of the kings of France; the works of Samuel Usque and Moses de Rossi; in the seventeenth century, the works of David Gans, of Daniel Konforte, of Miguel di Barrios; and, in the eighteenth century, of Jechiel Heilprin and others.

Meanwhile a vast material reflecting this high civilisation is at hand, scattered throughout the great mass of manuscripts and early printed books which time and the ignorant, bigoted persecutors have spared us; and it may be slipping from under our grasp, to the inestimable loss of humanity. There are living among us still men to whom Hebrew in all its dialects is a living language, as ancient Greek was to the earliest dwellers in ancient Hellas. And it is to be feared that this intimate knowledge and familiarity with the language and the thought will die out with these men.

I have before me a book on the *History of Jewish Literature*, by Gustav Karpeles, in German, which has appeared within the last few years. Though in these two volumes the author cannot aspire to completeness, the impression which, both for extent and quality, the summary account of the literary works of the Jewish people produces in us is one of deep regret, if not of revolt, that we should have been deprived for so long of vast treasures which might have added to the elevation and refinement of civilised nations.

He has subdivided the whole of Jewish literature into six periods:

The first reaches down to the year 200 B.C., and comprises ancient Hebrew writings during the period of national independence, which forms the groundwork for the whole of the subsequent literature. This is the period of Biblical literature.

The second period extends to the year A.D. 100, and marks the junction between the Hebrew and the Hellenic world. Most of the works are written in Greek. This is the Judæo-Hellenistic period.

The third period, more extensive as regards time, stretches over nearly a thousand years. It contains chiefly the work on the two Talmuds, and the literature related to them, though other sciences and even poetry are developed. This is the period of Talmudic literature.

The fourth period, extending over three hundred years, forms the second golden age of Jewish literature. The Jews took part in all spheres of the intellectual life of the Arabs; they wrote in Arabic, Hebrew, and Aramaic. They developed general literature and poetry, philosophy and grammar, astronomy and medicine, exegesis and theology. Rhyme and prosody of the Arabs often lend their form, and there is produced the flower of Neo-Hebraic poetry which lasts for more than a century. It is chiefly in North Africa, Spain, and Italy that the work of this period is localised; while in France and Germany we find that Biblical criticism and the study of law are cultivated.

The name which Karpeles assigns to this period, reaching to the beginning of the thirteenth century, is the Judæo-Arabico-Spanish literature.

The fifth period has no very definite character. It lasts about five centuries, down to the point marked by the life of Moses Mendelssohn. The dispersion of the Jews after the new Spanish exile, the invention of the printing-press, the revival of letters, all exert a direct influence. The weakened general intellectual vitality of the Jews of this age makes it possible for the Cabbala with its mysticism and magic to gain in influence. At the same time the study of the law is more and more extended and represses poetry and philosophy. The language is not a definite one, unless one were to call that Talmudic idiom, the mixture of Hebrew and Aramaic, a definite language. This is called Rabbinic literature.

The last period begins towards the close of the eighteenth century, and in it the Jews of Germany take the lead. Accordingly, the language of the most important product of this period is German; but of course, as in all periods, great works are published in Hebrew as well as in other living languages. In this era, which might be called the revival of science, the character, form, and contents of literature naturally also change. There is an aftermath of poetry, and what is commonly called 'Belletristic,' while the sciences are highly developed. This is called the period of modern Jewish literature.

The number of great names, of poets and men of letters, which we meet with in this account, the variety of works, the excellence of quality which is ascribed to them by those who are capable of appreciating their merits, will bear comparison with any national literature of which we know. And it is not only in contributions to religious and philosophical thought, nor in those which have influenced the advancement of science, that this literature abounds : it is also rich in pure literature ; in poetry, lyrical, didactic, epic, devotional ; in the drama, in the novel, and in satire. And these works are not only in Hebrew and Arabic, but, to a great part, in Spanish and in all other living tongues. Surely we who are the sons of European civilisation have a claim to these treasures, and the question is, how can they best be made accessible ?

The first duty in this direction lies with

the Jews themselves. Not that there are not learned men among them, rabbis and others, who have always, and especially of late years, brought their learning to bear upon this task. But not enough is done, nor is it done with sufficient method. Every Jewish rabbi in charge of the numerous congregations all over the civilised globe, all those connected with the synagogue, or general students of their religious history—in short, all those who are intimately conversant with the Hebrew language and capable of dealing with its literature, ought to contribute their mite to the consummation of this great aim.

It was the pride of the Jewish rabbis of old that they were not purely priests; they were teachers, learned in their law and in their literature, and thus took the place of a schoolmaster or a professor of the university. They even practised some trade or profession, which was so wholesome in counteracting the one-sidedness to which the lofty vocation of priest and teacher may lead, always in danger of producing a diseased state of the mind and of the character. It is well to remember the injunction of Rabbi Gamaliel III. in the third century A.D.: 'It is beautiful to be occupied with the law if one also carries on secular work. The exertion in both spheres does not allow sin to hold up its head. Knowledge of the law without craft or trade at last goes under and drags sin after it.' But, sad to say, this tradition has not always been preserved. With the example of the Christian priesthood about them, and the unconscious influence which such surroundings produce, the Jewish rabbi has often developed into the Jewish priest, and finds his duties limited by those of a ritual and 'pastoral' nature.

There ought to be a great congress of rabbis and learned Jews, not for the purpose of theological disputation, not to discuss ritual and church organisation, but to organise the division of the great literary labour, to elaborate and to make accessible to the civilised world the treasures which we know are there, though hidden under a thick crust of unintelligible language. Each one of these rabbis, students, or doctors in the law ought to undertake the editing or translation of some portion of this intellectual cosmos. Not only those who are learned or who are Hebrew scholars, but even a simple Jew who is merely familiar with the modern patois called 'Judisch-deutsch,' and is possessed of literary taste, might give us some of the treasures couched in this inaccessible dialect. The Jewish societies and alliances ought to ignore the ephemeral movements which are now directed against them, and ought to divest themselves of all militant character, even though they be only on the defensive : but all their united efforts ought to flow into peaceful channels and be directed towards the preservation and diffusion of the intellectual wealth which Judaism is keeping to itself, though it does not even enjoy the fruits. Here also lies the domain of the publication societies, which ought not to be directed by any practical purpose of this militant character, but rather by the purely theoretical motive of publishing works which, under ordinary circumstances, would not commend themselves to the business publisher. They ought not to accept works which, in their general scope and character, do not come into the region of pure research, but can, and ought to, find their place in the general competition of modern books.

This is the attitude which the Jews ought to hold with regard to this great task. But I maintain that the question does not concern the Jews only, but is universal in its scope and interest. This intellectual life and these intellectual treasures do not now belong only to the Jews—as little as the life, literature, and art of ancient Hellas belong to modern Greece. They belong to us all. Ancient Hellenic thought and life have manifestly and avowedly been incorporated into the whole civilised consciousness; and I claim the opportunity of doing the same by the mediæval life of the Jews. To this end the action of the Jews themselves which I have just recommended is but a preliminary stage; but the real channels through which this intellectual life is to flow into the widened spheres of modern culture are the universities and the learned societies.

In a few universities there are chairs of Talmudic and Rabbinic literature; but these have not yet found their proper sphere and activity, nor are they fulfilling their essential function. As far as I can ascertain, this is not so much due to any remissness on the part of those who hold those chairs, but rather to the general want of a knowledge and understanding of the facts which I am endeavouring to impress in this chapter. As it is, the teaching seems to appeal almost exclusively to the theological faculty, whereas it really belongs to the department of humanistics. The students who, by predisposition, consider themselves to be appealed to by such a study are almost exclusively of the theological faculty, a few candidates to priesthood in the various Christian sects, or those who mean to become rabbis. It may lap over into the humanistic studies; but it will then only be in its relation to Oriental languages. Now the faculties to which such a study ought really to appeal would be those of philosophy, history, and literature. With regard to philology, this study does not only concern the section of Oriental languages, but it may also enter into the domain of mediæval language.[1] After what has already been said, I need not dwell any longer upon the important relation which mediæval Judaism holds to mediæval history and mediæval literature, and we must hope that distinguished students of this department, not biassed by any Jewish

[1] The Jewish-German patois to which I have referred is spread all over Europe. There is no doubt that in it are contained many forms and remnants of early German; and it would, for instance, repay the student of Germanic language to make a careful investigation of this dialect for the new light it may throw upon the earlier history of the German tongue.

proclivities, will give their careful attention to this unexplored domain.

Finally, I would advocate the formation of Hebraic societies, corresponding to the Hellenic societies which now exist in most civilised centres of Western life. These are to have no direct relation to the Jewish societies and alliances which already exist; for their aim is to be purely scientific, literary, and artistic, without any admixture of racial or quasi-racial tendencies. Their relation to these narrower organisations might possibly be one of history, such as we find in the history of the Hellenic antiquarian societies. The first antiquarian societies, which have since done so much for the revival of interest in the classical world and the extension of our knowledge concerning it, also had their origin to a great extent in historical patriotism and in local association. The first classical antiquarian society started in Rome during the Renaissance was to a great extent moved by the desire to prove or to maintain the relationship between the great classical past and the Roman Italy of the day. But this narrow though stimulating aim was soon merged in the broader prospect which such intellectual effort opened out to the awakened intelligence of the peoples of the Renaissance. And now the nations of Germanic origin have done as much as, if not more than, those of Romance origin to preserve and to revivify the refining and ennobling influence of the great classical past.

In the same way, no doubt, the existing Hebrew organisations have done and are doing good work in this direction as regards mediæval Jewish civilisation. They are no doubt collecting, and thereby preserving, the scattered remnants of this literature, and, as was shown by the interesting exhibit in the Paris Exhibition of 1878, and in subsequent exhibitions, they have done much towards the preservation of Jewish antiquities. But the whole of this intellectual and moral sphere must be widened out. All civilised people of our time have a right, if not a duty, to share in the work; and free from any limitation and admixture of religion, race, or caste, we may hope to see the organisation and growth of such broader Hebraic antiquarian societies to supplement the flourishing Hellenic societies to which we owe so much. We shall then be nearer to completing our intellectual horizon-line as regards the past, which shows gaps in important points; and within this horizon the intellectual and moral life which is near at hand, under our feet, and before our eyes, will be made more fertile and more beautiful by the final union in harmony of what ought never to be divorced—Hebraism and Hellenism.

Rabbi Jochanan, in the third century A.D., recommended that Jewish girls should be allowed to learn the beautiful Greek characters, as this language was an ornament to womankind. His appreciation for Hellenism is summed up in the figurative language of his prayer:

'The beauty of Japhet [the type of Hellenism] is to dwell in the tents of Shem' [Hebraism].

VI

MONEY AND THE JEWS

THE preceding chapters must have made us realise the spiritual tendencies of the Jews and the predominance of the spiritual element in their lives. Still there is current the common view that they are materialistic in their tendency, and that money-greed is one of their chief characteristics. This I believe to be untrue, and I shall endeavour to prove it.

As far as modern times are concerned, I suppose it is a common error, chiefly due to the fact that there are so many among them who are prosperous in the worldly conditions of their life. Yet we must not forget that since the downfall of chivalry, as a matter of fact, the only visible outward sign of excellence, the 'common denominator' of value, in so far as it makes itself physically perceptible, is money. We may deplore this or not, we do not make it the less a fact. In this respect we are no doubt living in a great and all-important transition in our time, and we are all suffering from the dualism in our moral consciousness which is the natural outcome of this transition. I hold this dualism to be one of the central causes of the unrest and the pessimism which rob the spirit of our age of that peace and repose requiring, above all things, the singleness and clearness of purpose, the complete moral approbation granted to our main incentives of action and effort. With the downfall of feudalism and its common code of success which brought distinction, the general energies of men were led into economical channels, while we have not as yet established those clear and universally recognisable standards of democratic social distinction which should take the place of previous rewards offered to noble ambition by the worldly powers. But, on the other hand, our age has strongly felt that this economical test of value is not sufficient—nay, that it may be degrading and pernicious. And there is thus a disturbing contradiction, a revolt of our higher moral and ideal aspirations in conflict with the universal and valid impulses guiding our activity and regulating our aims in the daily exercise of our duty as bread-winners. We are slowly working out these problems either by the violent forms of socialistic agitation, or by the violent opposition to this in the individualistic direction, or by moderating influences of compromise, or, finally, by the single and unconscious efforts of each man who does his best to spiritualise the material struggle for life by the introduction of moral, religious, and charitable elements. But as yet, to say the least, but few among us have clearly declared that the acquisition of wealth within the limits laid down by the law is an unworthy endeavour, indicative of a low and mercenary spirit.

After a comparatively long and thorough study of the Jews and the Jewish question, I now venture to say that they are not usually predisposed to love money as such; that they, on the contrary, if I should summarise them in one word, tend to be a nation of thinkers, and that thought has ever brought them the highest consideration; that the actual facts of their history show this; and, finally, that their association with finance and money business is accidental, not essential to them.

I may at once anticipate the proving of this

thesis by an observation of facts which are
close at hand and under our eyes. While in
Europe the great financial enterprises, or those
of a speculative character, may be in a large
proportion in the hands of the Jews, owing
to the circumstances of their history, in the
United States of America, the home of modern
financiering and speculation, this is not the
case. The great financiers and promoters
in that country, the millionaires who have
amassed their fortunes by the mere manipula-
tion of capital, are chiefly Americans of British
extraction. The Jews of America, on the other
hand (I am here ignoring the large proportion
of poorer Jews), are chiefly representatives of
what I should call legitimate commerce and
industry, importers and exporters of goods,
and manufacturers. Moreover, the evidence
which I have collected from unbiassed people
with regard to the Jewish business men in
America tends to show that they are comparatively possessed of the higher business
integrity. Now the fact that the Jews have
not in any way controlled the world of finance
and speculation in America (in spite of the
predisposition which they might have inherited from their recent European traditions

and the connections which they would have found from the very outset) is negatively due to the fact that in America there exists for them no tradition of any restriction with regard to their occupation which might have forced them into this sphere of finance. And it helps to show the truth of what I shall endeavour to prove by other testimony,— namely, that this occupation is accidental and not essential to the Jewish people.

In the Middle Ages, down to our own times, the Jew was restricted in his occupations, and the superior members of this community had open to them but three spheres of activity : commerce, finance, or the profession of medicine. Yet, in spite of what I have just said with regard to the change in our views and moral estimate with which we are at this moment struggling, it is a mistake to think that in the past, and in the Middle Ages, commerce and finance were bad in themselves, and that the world does not, on the contrary, owe to them the greatest debt. In the Middle Ages the people were too ignorant to become merchants and financiers—nay, they were even frequently too low in their civilisation to have evolved the needs for these economical institutions. Charlemagne and many of his followers felt their necessity and realised the great advantage which they would bring. But commerce and finance required qualifications which could not be found among the serfs and even the knights of those ages. It demanded the knowledge of languages, wide views, a mobile, constructive imagination, and, above all, integrity.

I believe that the influence of commerce upon the development of morals has not been properly perceived or felt. More than any worldly institution it appears to me to have contributed to the creation of *abstract* morality with regard to truth, in contradistinction to *personal* morality and veracity. Whoever has lived in countries into which commerce has not as yet penetrated, especially in the East, must have realised the total absence of the sense for an abstract duty to truth such as stamps our moral consciousness. One often meets with instances of supreme personal fidelity and faithfulness; but it is through the channels of love and gratitude, through the emotions, and not through the unswerving action of an abstract belief in the necessity of truth independent of any personal regard or affection. There may be many causes for this fact; but it appears to me that the difference is to be ascribed in a considerable degree to the presence or absence of the influence of commerce in contradistinction to barter. This form of commerce has effectually introduced into the regions in which it has become dominant the idea of abstract veracity. The extensive transactions of such commerce cannot be controlled by the eyes of the participants; it thus depends upon faith in the truthfulness of the parties who may be separated from one another by the mountains and seas. And the more complicated this commercial system grows, the greater grows the need for this veracity.

The Jews thus performed a definite function as merchants in the life of mediæval Europe, and wealth accrued to them from it. The same holds good with finance. They were the bankers and financiers of the Middle Ages. The word *usury* may really cover a multitude of sins; but we must take heed lest it do not cover and smother entirely a number of virtues. Whatever we may feel now, the fact remains that usury in the Middle Ages was the natural and normal form of our banking business; and that through it commerce was developed out of the rudimentary barter stage. This commercial advancement did much for the spread of civilisation. We must also remember that even pawnbrokery was a legitimate, and, in some respects, beneficial form of business in the earlier days, sometimes the monopoly of States and princes, and that the three balls of the modern pawnbroker represent the arms of the Medici family. But we can equally understand how those benefited by this sphere of utility which was left open to the intellectual superiority of the Jews should dislike the position of the debtor more than that of the creditor, and should heap the odium of their displeasure, and even hatred, upon those to whom they were thus indebted.

The main functions of these Jews, so far as it was not purely commercial, was that of bringing capital and labour together, and, in so far, of raising the civilisation in these countries. They were what the bankers are now. Such was their influence, for instance, in England towards the close of the twelfth and the beginning of the thirteenth century.

' In Angevin England,' says a late writer, ' it became impossible to obtain the capital for any

large scheme of building or organisation unless
the projectors had the capital themselves.

'Here was the function which the Jew could
perform in England of the twelfth century,
which was just passing economically out of the
stage of barter. Capital was wanted in particular for the change of architecture from
wood to stone for the better classes, and
especially for the erection of castles and monasteries. The Jews were, indeed, the first in
England to possess dwelling-houses built with
stone, probably for purposes of protection as
well as for comfort. And for a specimen of
their influence on monastic architecture, we
have it on record that no less than nine Cister-
cian monasteries of the north country were
built by moneys lent by the great Aaron of
Lincoln, who also boasted that he had built the
shrine of St. Alban. It was chiefly, then, the
smaller barons and the monasteries that needed
the capital of the Jews, and it is characteristic
enough that their chief persecutors came from
precisely these two classes.

'The Church prohibition of "usury" would
have been ineffective if the State had not followed suit. If the usurer had merely to fear
the spiritual terrors of the Church, the prac-

tice might not have been very greatly checked. But the State followed suit by confiscating the chattels of a usurer who died in his sin, and applied the provision quite impartially to Jew or Christian. This provision brought about a curious result when there came to exist a class of men like the Jews of Angevin England, whose sole function was to be usurers or capitalists. The State as represented by the king became the universal legatee of the whole Jewry, and thus was brought into immediate connection, a sort of sleeping partnership, with Jewish usury.

'The result of the Church's attitude towards Jews and towards usury was to put the king into a peculiar relation towards his Jewish subjects. The Church kept them out of all other pursuits but that of usury, which it branded as infamous; the State followed suit, and confiscated the estates of all usurers dying as such. Hence, as a Jew could only be a usurer, his estate was always potentially the king's, and could be dealt with by the king as if it were his own. Yet, strange to say, it was not to the king's interest to keep the Jew's wealth in his own hands, for he (the king), as a good Christian, could not get usury for it,

while the Jew could very soon double and
treble it, since the absence of competition
enabled him to fix the rate of interest very
high, rarely less than forty per cent., often as
much as eighty. As the Jew might die before
the debt was due and the king be then content
to take a much smaller sum as a composition
for the debt, it was often the debtor's interest
to keep the debt standing. The usury was in
the nature of a bet against the Jew's life. The
only useful function the Jew could perform
towards both king and people was to be as rich
as possible, just as the larger the capital of a
bank the more valuable the part it plays in the
world of commerce. No wonder the expression " rich as a Jew " passed into a proverb ;
as applied to the English Jew of the twelfth
century, it was as tautologous as saying " rich
as a bank."

'The king reaped the benefit of these riches
in several ways. One of his main functions
and main source of income was selling justice,
and Jews were among his best customers.
Then he claimed from them, as from his other
subjects, fines and amerciaments for all the
events of life. The Pipe-rolls contain entries
of fines paid by Jews to marry, not to marry,

to become divorced, to go a journey across the sea, to become partners with another Jew [1]— in short, for all the decisive events of life. And, above all, the king got frequent windfalls from the heirs of deceased Jews, who paid heavy reliefs to have their fathers' charters and debts, of which, as we have seen, they could make more profitable use than the king, to whom the Jews' property escheated, not *quâ* Jew, but *quâ* usurer. In the case of Aaron of Lincoln the king did not disgorge at all at his death, but kept in his own hands the large treasures, lands, houses, and debts of the great financier. He appears to have first organised the Jewry, and made the whole of the English Jews his agents throughout the country. Aaron's treasures were lost at sea, but his debts amounted to some £20,000, more than half the king's income, and required a special branch of the Exchequer, the *Scaccarium Aaronis*, with two treasurers and two clerks to look after them for many years thereafter.

'This great windfall, which occurred in 1187, must have opened the eyes of the king's officials to the profitable source of income that

---

[1] There was a special reason why the king claimed compensation for a partnership between Jews. Debts to the firm would not fall into his hands when one of the partners died.

lay in Jewish usury; three years later they learned the dangers to which this source was liable. The *émeutes* of 1189-90, culminating in the York massacre, had as one of their objects the destruction of the deeds and charters of the Jews; in York they were burned in the minster. The loss sustained by the king led to the organisation of the Jewry in 1194, when the "Ordinances of the Jewry" were promulgated; these provided for a full record of all Jewish business to be kept in the king's hands, so that he might know exactly how much each Jew was worth, and how much he could extract from him. The Exchequer of the Jews of the thirteenth century, with its Star-chamber, devoted to the *Shetars* of the Hebrew usurers, grew out of the "Ordinances of the Jewry," but lies beyond the limits of our present purview.[1]

'For, in addition to these quasi-regular and normal sources of income from his Jews, the king claimed from them (again as from his other subjects) various contributions from time to time under the names of gifts and tallages. And here he certainly seems, on occasion at

[1] See the excellent paper of Dr. C. Gross on the subject in papers of the Anglo-Jewish Historical Exhibition, 1888.

least, to have exercised an unfavourable discrimination in his demands from the Jews. In 1187, the year of Aaron of Lincoln's death, he took a tenth from the rest of England, which yielded £70,000, and a quarter from the Jews, which gave as much as £60,000. In other words, the Jews were reckoned to have, at that date, one-quarter of the movable wealth of the kingdom (£240,000 against £700,000 held by the rest).'[1]

No doubt the rate of interest was inordinately high; but it could not well be otherwise. The share which the kings and other rulers exacted, and the precariousness of the business, owing to the arbitrary robberies of the State itself, made this necessary. In spite of this, the beneficial influence of the Jews in the economical life of Europe during the Middle Ages must be acknowledged and ought never to be ignored.

Charlemagne marks the beginning of the Occidental civilisation of Europe as opposed to the Byzantine empire. We have already seen how he valued the intellectual life of the

[1] This quotation is from a book which has just appeared: *The Jews of Angevin England*, by J. Jacobs, London, 1893.

Jews; but he prized none the less the civilising influence which the extension of commerce through them might have upon Europe. The nobles in his time followed the profession of war, while the lower classes consisted of artisans, the peasantry, or serfs. The Jews were needed by him to supply the needed class, and he conferred upon them privileges corresponding to those granted subsequently to great commercial companies. They not only benefited the country in which they lived through their commerce, but also through the introduction of manufactories. Thus, in the twelfth century, the Jews brought the silk industry into Greece, especially at Thebes; in the thirteenth century they opened out the agricultural wealth of the districts of the lower Danube, Vistula, and on either side of the Karpathians.

The advantage which the Jews had been to Spain became most manifest after their expulsion. In spite of the robbery which was practised upon them, it is estimated that they carried away with them thirty million ducats; but what was still more important was the fact that Spain lost the twentieth part of its inhabitants —the most energetic portion of its population—

not only capitalists, merchants, agriculturists, physicians, and learned men, but also artisans, armourers, and metal-workers of all kinds. Towns were deserted, and all enterprise came to a stand-still. Notwithstanding the acquisition of so many wealthy colonies, Spain from that day on became more and more impoverished. All Europe, even the Parliament of Paris, charged Ferdinand with the folly of losing so useful a class of his people, quite apart from the cruelty of the act. The Sultan Bayazid of Turkey invited the Jews to settle in his country, and said: "You call Ferdinand a wise monarch—he who has impoverished his country and enriched our own?"

Wherever these exiled Jews settled prosperity accrued to the whole region. At the end of the fifteenth century Jerusalem had seventy Jewish families; at the beginning of the sixteenth it had fifteen hundred. From having been one of the lowest and filthiest places, under the leadership of Obadja da Bertinoro, it became clean, beautiful, and thriving. Salonichi grew into a city with more Jewish than other inhabitants, and the result was its great prosperity and commerce. Every wise country recognised them as a blessing. In Poland in the sixteenth century, the king and the nobles feared their emigration to Turkey. In this kingdom there were only five hundred Christian merchants to thirty-two hundred who were Jews; while the Jewish artisans, gold and silver smiths, blacksmiths, and weavers were three times as numerous as the Christian. Ancona, in Italy, was made through the Jews a thriving seaport, so that Francesco della Rovere I., Duke of Urbino, invited the learned Molch to settle at Pesero, in order to attract thither the wealthy Jews of Ancona, and thus benefit his whole country. The Duke Ercole II. of Ferrara strongly urged them to settle in his domains. We have already examined their position in Holland; but it must be remembered that this country, from having been one of the poorest in Europe, before the immigration of the Jews, still further impoverished by its heroic war against Spain, began, from that moment, to take one of the foremost places in the world's commerce. They needed the capital and the commercial knowledge and connections of the Jews expelled from Spain, and it was in great part due to these that the trade to the East and West Indies was brought to them.

This was universally recognised at the time, and all wise monarchs desired them to settle in their country. So King Christian IV. of Denmark wrote a letter to the head of the Amsterdam congregation asking him to encourage some of his flock to settle in Denmark, and promising them freedom of religious worship and other privileges. The Duke of Savoy invited them to Nizza, and the Duke of Modena to Reggio.

Nor is it a mere coincidence that with their settlement as merchants in England British commerce took its great rise in modern times. In Menasse Ben Israel's address to Cromwell, the fact of this influence of the Jews is directly impressed; he refers to the exchange business of the Jews, to their commerce in diamonds, cochineal, indigo, wines, and oils; to the fact that the Maranos of Spain intrusted their capital to the Dutch Jews. In the Republic of Venice, Luzzato showed statistically that the Jews of the republic brought to it more than two hundred and fifty thousand ducats a year, gave labour to four thousand workmen, produced the home goods cheaply, and introduced goods from distant countries.

Modern Germany in more recent times owes,

perhaps, more to the Jews than any other country. Besides the beneficial influence which they had upon the spiritual elevation of Germany out of its humiliating position in the last century, and the awakening of their national heroism by such men as Moses Mendelssohn, they are further indebted to them for the increase of their national prosperity. In 1755, Mendelssohn, in his *Philosophical Conversations*, blamed the Germans that they did not recognise their own national genius, and bowed down to French taste. How un-German and servile the courts were in this respect is universally known. I can remember myself, when I first visited Germany, the impression it produced upon me to find that the language of the courts and of the aristocracy was still French. The Jews of Germany have proved themselves patriots in every respect, and the wealth of such cities as Hamburg, Frankfort, Berlin, and Nuremberg is to a great extent due to their influence. Especially through the settlement of so many of their merchants in the United States of America, the commerce and industry of Germany in its relation to the United States has received the strongest impulse.

It may be held at this moment that commerce and financiering occupy too prominent a place in modern economical life, and that their advance must now be checked. But this does not affect the great utility which they have had in the past, and hence ought not to affect the gratitude and consideration due to the Jews for having fostered it. Commerce and finance and speculation have not for many years been the monopoly of the Jews, and any opposition to the spread of these, by legislation or otherwise, is untrue and defeats its own end if it hides its purpose and fans its violence under the cloak of national and racial prejudice.

The restrictions in the free choice of their occupation drove the Jews into mercantile pursuits; but I maintain that they are not naturally predisposed to them; that their submission has not produced in them as an essential characteristic the money-greed with which they are ignorantly charged.

The impression which the study of their past produces leads me to believe that without such compulsory restrictions on the part of their enemies, the ideals of their life are essentially found in agricultural pursuits, on the one hand, and in scholarship on the other.

The ancient Jews of the Old Testament were chiefly an agricultural or a nomadic people. It is under the shade of their vineyards or their olive-trees, or in the tent of the shepherd, that the picture of happy life is localised by them. Ranke speaks of the earliest tribes as "a wandering tribal army of one single caste, all of them warriors; the portion of them selected for the service of the sanctuary even held no pre-eminent position."

Those tribes who lived on the sea-coast no doubt were occupied with navigation and commerce, and herein joined the Phœnicians; but the main body, living in the interior, were an agricultural people. The gardens of Babylon, the elaborate system of canals for the irrigation of this country, marked it as one of the most fertile districts, most highly and intelligently cultivated, of the ancient world.

This essential feature of the earliest Israelites maintained itself in the Middle Ages in those Eastern Jewish tribes to whom reference has been made in Chapter III. In Europe, too, in the Middle Ages, down to the time of Charlemagne, wherever they were not prevented by the tyrannical majority among whom they lived, they were also the possessors and tillers of land, besides being tradespeople and navigators.

The sayings and teachings of their leaders and wise men directly bear out this fact. With few exceptions these teachers and priests were not paid. The changes in the practice of their learned men corresponded to the change from the life of the Socratic and earlier philosophers to the custom of the sophists in Greece, though I do not believe that it ever reached so complete a development in the mercenary direction among the Jews. Some of the most celebrated of their teachers and leaders were themselves farmers, taking active part in agricultural work; so the great Huna, who continued his agricultural labours even when he was chief in the third century. Wealth derived from field labour seems even to have been prized more highly than when it sprang from trade, as is borne out by the aphorism of Rabbi Arica, addressed to his son : 'Better a small measure from the fields than a large one from the storehouse' (trade or commerce).

I cannot find a trace which would justify the opinion that the Jews ever were characterised by the love of money for its own sake. I should say that the typical miser is a rare

figure among them.   The love of money
appears to have been only the love of that
which money brings; and among these desirable
objects I should say that their tastes led more
towards the spiritual than the material region.
Negatively, I should say that those people care
least for money, as such, who are most willing
to part with it for charitable purposes.   That
the Jews are pre-eminent in their charities,
from the earliest times down to our days, cannot be controverted.   One of the causes of the
admiration which Julianus Apostata had for
the Jews was their charity to the poor, so that
none of their community was ever allowed to
suffer want.   I will give two characteristic
instances of the life of the rich during the
third century, as related by Graetz:

Huna (born 220, died 297) was chief of the
school of Sura and the most prominent teacher
of his age.   Although related to the Exilarch
of the period, he was not himself wealthy.
The small farm which he possessed he cultivated himself; and he was wont to say, when
called upon to act as judge, 'Send me a sub-
stitute to work my field and I will be your
judge.'   He often returned from his work
with his spade over his shoulder, and, walking

thus, he often met the richest man of Babylon, a certain Chama Bar Amilai. This wealthy man was also the most liberal and charitable man in the community. It was said of him that he resembled Father Abraham in having attained the ideal in the performance of the Jewish virtue, to be the father of the poor. Day and night the cooks of his house were at work, and there were doors on every side into which the necessitous could enter, and whoever was hungry was satisfied. When Chama was walking he kept his hand in his money-bag, so that a shy pauper should not be placed in the trying position of waiting for his alms. During the famine he caused wheat and barley to be placed at night-time in the houses of those poor who were kept by shame from entering among the crowd of beggars. He was free from all pride, and whenever he met Huna returning home from his labour with his spade over his shoulder, he manifested his reverence in begging to carry the spade for him. Huna would never submit to this, for he said Chama was not accustomed to carry a spade in Babylon, and that for this reason he would not allow him to carry it there. Huna came into great property, and then he gave part of the proceeds of the farm to the field labourers—an early form of co-operation. He made the noblest use of his fortune. When from the Syrian desert the cyclones came, he would be carried about in his litter and inspect the houses of Sura, and would cause every unsound wall to be torn down and repaired, paying for it in case the owner was not able to do so. During meal-time he had all the doors of his house opened, and made the announcement, "Whoever is in want, let him satisfy himself." Among the eight hundred pupils who attended his lectures he sustained all those who were poor.

The innumerable instances of magnificent charity to their persecuted brothers during the Inquisition need not be enumerated. But this charity was not, nor has it ever been, restricted to their own race and nation. I believe that, considering the cruelty with which they have been treated by Christians for ages, vindictiveness cannot in any way be considered one of their characteristics. During the Hussite war, in 1421, the imperial army massacred the Jews as the Crusaders had done. But when they suffered defeat at Saaz and were driven through the country in confusion, many of these soldiers, who had sworn death to the Jews, came starved to their doors and were fed by them. When, in the sixteenth century, King Sebastian of Portugal, with the flower of his army, was defeated in Africa, and the Portuguese prisoners were sold as slaves in the market at Fez, the knights and nobles considered it good fortune if they were bought by the grandchildren of the Jews whom their ancestors had so cruelly persecuted, for they were sure of kind treatment from them. But I hardly think I need add other instances; the contrary seems to me never to have been seriously maintained.

If, now, we turn to the mediæval history of the relation of the Jews to the princes and the ruling classes, it seems to me beyond all doubt to be the fact that the money-greed was on the side of the Christian oppressors, and not on that of the Jews. The relation which these rulers had to the Jews was that of a sleeping, unworking partner in the financial transactions of the Jew—nay, in every craft or trade which they practised—without any fairness of contract on their part, generally coupled with the most cruel robbery. I cannot recall which of the great historians of the Middle Ages it is—

I believe it is Dr. Stubbs, the Bishop of Chester—who has said that the greed for money is one of the most striking features in the history of the Middle Ages. This must impress itself upon every student who goes deeper into the history of that age. And this is so in spite of what I have said concerning the ideal standards of public distinction, of chivalry as opposed to that of modern times. For these standards remained, however much the individual actions of even the school-book heroes may have belied them. I here give but a few instances, to which many more might be added.

Louis VII. of France was friendly to the Jews. He had hardly closed his eyes when his son, Philip Auguste, feeling oppressed by the want of money, turned upon the Jews to remedy this evil. Though in France at that time comparatively few trafficked in money and though bishops, counts, and barons intervened in their favour and begged to have them remain, they were expelled from France in the twelfth century, and in the following manner:

On January 19, 1180, without any definite charge against them, he caused all the Jews in France to be captured and to be thrown

T

into prison while they were assembled in their
synagogues for Sabbath worship. He had
counted upon a heavy ransom from them, and
after they had paid fifteen hundred marks in
silver they were set at liberty. But this was
only the prelude to the tragedy. Before the
expiration of that same year he declared all
debts of Christians to Jews cancelled; but took
care to claim one-fifth of the debts from which
they were thus released *in toto* from the Christian debtors. The hermit of Vincennes
encouraged him in this action, holding that to
rob the Jews of their wealth was a good work
in the eyes of God. Not satisfied with thus
having made beggars of them, he put out an
edict shortly after this that all the Jews of
the North of France had to leave the country
between April and June of the year 1181.
They were only allowed to sell their movable
property, while their land, vineyards, barns,
and wine-presses should go to the king. The
synagogues were turned into churches. But a
very small proportion of the Jews escaped
this fate through conversion. The charges
which were brought against the Jews of
murdering children and of extortion in money
matters were absolutely unfounded.

With Henry III. in England the Jews met
with a similar fate, and could only find protection through the money paid to the king.
In the thirteenth century, when the German
Jews wished to escape oppression under the
leadership of the Rabbi of Rothenburg, and
were about to emigrate to Persia, where there
was a prospect of greater freedom, the Emperor
Rudolph had the Rabbi thrown into prison at
Ensisheim. He was well treated in prison,
for the emperor was not bent upon punishing
him; he only wished to retain him in his
country because he feared that through a large
emigration of the Jews the imperial treasury
might lose a great portion of its income.
Meanwhile the Christian citizens of Mayence
and of other cities had already seized upon
the houses and lands of the Jews who had
started to emigrate; but the emperor claimed
these as his own, and took them away. The
Jews of Germany then offered the emperor
twenty thousand marks in silver if the
murderers of the Jews of Oberwesel and
Boppart were brought to justice and Rabbi
Meïr released. The emperor accepted the
money, but did not carry out the conditions,
and Rabbi Meïr was kept in prison for five

years. Let it be that the emperor wished to get further sums out of the Jews, or that, as is said, the rabbi did not wish to be liberated in this manner (for he feared that seizing upon rabbis might be used as a further means of blackmail); at all events, the rabbi remained in prison for a further five years, and died there, his body being left without interment by the emperor's successor, until a Jew of Frankfort, Süskind Alexander Wimpfen, succeeded in procuring the corpse for a high sum, and then buried the rabbi at Worms.

In the fourteenth century Philip IV. (Le Beau), who had before protected the Jews, needing money (the popular song of the time said 'that not the chicken in the pot was saved from the clutches of the king'), gave a secret order to all his officers in the whole empire to seize upon all the Jews in his kingdom on the same day; and while they were celebrating their day of atonement, men, women, and children were thus thrown into prison. They were then told that, leaving behind them their property, as well as the certificates of debts, they were to leave the country within a month. The cause for this cruel action was, in the first place, the greed of money; but another circumstance contributed to it. The German emperor, Albrecht, had demanded of Philip the kingdom of Arles; further, the crown of thorns of Christ, which he was supposed to have in his possession; and, finally, to cede to him his rights over the Jews, which belonged to him as the successor of the Emperor Vespasian, Titus, and Charlemagne; that is, to give him a part of the hard-earned bread of the Jews. Philip is said to have consulted his jurists as to these rights over the Jews, and, as they were held to belong to the emperor, he conceived the idea of stripping them naked of their possessions and sending them abroad. And thus over a hundred thousand people were expelled from the land which their ancestors had held even in the time of the Roman Republic, long before the advent of the Franks and of Christianity. The king's officers only allowed them the clothes which they wore and rations for one day.

About the same time a similar fate threatened them from Pope John XII., which was only averted by payment of twenty thousand ducats, through the intercession of their friend King Robert of Naples. The ground of this disturbance was that Sangisa, sister of the

Pope, had told her brother that she had seen Jews mocking the crucifix during a procession at Rome.

The cause of all this brutality was simply the money-greed of the torturers. When in the fourteenth century there was a general massacre of Jews in Germany during the black death, and there were all kinds of charges afloat against them, such as that they had poisoned the rivers of Germany, the honest Christian chronicler, Closener of Strasburg, says: 'Money was the poison which caused the Jews to be murdered.'

It is also significant to find, as regards the good these people did to the countries in which they lived, that in 1360 the Dauphin Charles of France issued a decree in which he invited the Jews to return to France with the consent of the higher and lower clergy, the higher and lower nobility, and all his citizens; that they should come for twenty years, freely follow their vocations, and possess land and houses. He granted them commercial privileges, legitimised the taking of interest up to eighty per cent. and protected their rights of pawn. He also bound himself not to burn the copies of their Bible and Talmud, as had so frequently been done. But, of course, they had to pay for this privilege in heavy taxes. Charles v. confirmed this right.

The stories making manifest this same greedy spirit on the part of the oppressors during the Spanish Inquisition and their expulsion from Spain are too numerous to dwell upon. But to take the most prominent case, that of Ferdinand and Isabella themselves. The Jews were here not punished on the ground of usury; but their religious influence is given as the main ground. Still, these monarchs were not deterred in their cruelty by the gains to their exchequer. It is characteristic that in expelling the Jews they generally allowed them to take away with them their goods, ' but no gold or silver coins, or goods of which the export was forbidden.' It was difficult for them to sell their property, and Ferdinand took possession of much of this, on the ground of covering their debts, and to satisfy the demands which the monasteries brought against them. The account of their sufferings in leaving their homes is heart-rending. They were cheated at every step, and they had to buy their right to pass through Portugal from the king of that country.

In 1598 the Emperor Maximilian revoked the protective privileges of the Jews, and permitted the town-council of Nuremberg to expel them. He granted this boon to the city of Nuremberg 'because of the fidelity which this city had ever shown to the imperial house;' but at the same time it was stipulated that all the houses, synagogues, and even the cemetery, should go to the imperial treasury.

In the seventeenth century one million two hundred thousand crusados were paid to Philip III. of Portugal to buy off the one hundred and fifty Maranos who were condemned by the Inquisition. Beziel Masserano had to arm himself with two thousand scudi when he went to Rome to beg from Pius IV. that the burning of the Talmud be discontinued. The baseness, coupled with the cruelty which meets one at every step in reading this portion of history, is positively nauseating; but the conclusion to which one invariably comes is that the money-greed was with the Christian rulers and their representatives of chivalry, and not with the Jews.

The spiritual and unmercenary character of Judaism becomes still more manifest when we recall the fact, to which reference has already been made in previous chapters, of the intellectual aspirations of the Jewish people as a people, and of the prestige which intellectual distinction and pursuits possess. I venture to say that among no people and in no period of history has the man of learning, the thinker, scholar, poet, and man of science had so high a position recognised by all portions of the community as is, and has been, the case among the Jews — I mean that these intellectual workers enjoyed as much prestige as any statesman, soldier, or man of wealth. And I believe that this striving after intellectual superiority is, of all, one of the most marked characteristics of the Jewish people. Though from the beginning they did not favour the one-sided development of study even among their rabbis, and though it was deemed advisable to preserve the normality of life so that the scholar and preacher should follow some worldly trade or profession, I hardly think that any other nation can show up in all its purity the type of the disinterested, unworldly student as can the Jews.

Many types can be found like Moses Narboni (Maestre Vidal), of the fourteenth century, who crossed the Pyrenees to Toledo and back again on foot, in order that he might learn, and losing all he had when the mob fell upon the community at Cevera during the black death—and, what he deplored most, all his books—quietly continued his work where he had left off; the purest type of philosopher, Spinoza, living in his garret, supporting his meagre bodily existence by grinding spectacle glasses while he wrote his immortal works, refusing brilliant offers of advancement—these types are far from having died out even in our days. Men like Bernays, the editor of *Heraclitus*, and many living scholars and students in Germany and elsewhere, might have served as prototypes of Carlyle's Teufelsdrockh and George Eliot's Mordecai. And the rarer these students grow in the universities of Germany and elsewhere, the greater relatively is their number among scores and hundreds of Jewish students and rabbis.

There may be—owing to their past history, there must needs be—many Jewish bankers; but I feel convinced that, if there were accurate statistics on this point, it would be found that in the proportion of those who devote themselves to spiritual and intellectual vocations

which are not considered to bring immediate
material gain, the modern Jews of Europe
would come out highest in the scale. Where-
ever they can, wherever they are allowed to do
so since the restrictions in the choice of work
have been taken from them, the Jews leave
the sphere of immediate money-making. It is
true there are not among them many farm
labourers ; but they have been kept from this
pursuit for centuries—the pursuit which needs
a peculiar physical and moral predisposition.
And now that we find that the farm labourers
are flocking to the large centres (not perhaps
to their own advantage, nor to that of the community), how can we in reason demand that
those who have not been bred in the tradition
of such occupation should at once run counter
to the general current and take to such work ?
Still, in those districts where they have been
allowed to till the land they have in modern
times soon manifested again this earliest predisposition of the ancient Hebrew people ; and
even the newly-formed agricultural communities are, according to all accounts, flourishing
and doing good work. And there can be
no doubt also that, for the Jews more
than for any other people, the encourage-

ment to agricultural pursuits is called for to rectify the physical and spiritual deficiencies which have been produced by the cruel oppression of their Christian contemporaries.

VII

M. ANATOLE LEROY-BEAULIEU AND THE JEWS

SINCE the foregoing chapters were written, a book has appeared by M. Anatole Leroy-Beaulieu, dealing with the whole of the Jewish question, entitled *Israel chez les Nations* (Paris, 1893). The attitude of the author is certainly not that of a Jew, though he brings to bear upon his discussion of the question an amount of sympathetic study of Jewish life and thought such as no other writer upon this subject has manifested. His point of view in dealing with the Jews is, as he says in his preface, that of a Christian and a Frenchman ('*Ce livre à été écrit par un Chrétien et un Français*'). If we add to these characteristics the eminent quali-ties of which the author proves himself to be possessed, as a man deeply imbued with the scientific spirit and with historical sympathy, we have indicated the main causes which have led to the production of so remarkable a book. As a true Christian, he has shown himself moved by a powerful impulse of charity. As a Frenchman, he is the inheritor of those liberal traditions which have ever led to the emancipation of the world by opposing all the injustice of sterile and selfish prerogatives, and by asserting the rights of man. As a man of science, he has conscientiously striven to discover the causes of phenomena, even those that are hidden, after he has determined what the phenomena are, and whether they lend themselves to scientific treatment. Finally, his historical sense has enabled him not only to sound the depths of life that has long since vanished from the scene of action, but also to enter into the thoughts, feelings, and memories of people still living, but living under entirely different conditions from those surrounding his own life, and resting upon traditions and customs, firmly rooted and even crystallised, with which his past has had no connection.

So much that is said by me has been seen and has been expressed by him, and his account is based upon so much wider an acquaintance with Jewish life, and is put in so beautiful a form, and in a style so concise, incisive, and still elegant, that at the first reading I considered my own work grotesquely superfluous beside such a presentation of the subject.

But upon second thought I have found that there are questions touched upon in my book which did not fall within the scope of the French author's work, and that these may be of some interest or importance. Furthermore, the fact that my point of departure in this examination of the Jewish question is not the same as his, may have led me in a few instances to conclusions differing somewhat from his own.

The main and fundamental difference between M. Leroy-Beaulieu and myself lies in the fact that, on the one hand, he distinctly and consciously deals with the subject as a Frenchman and a Christian, however scientific and sympathetic he may have been; while, on the other hand, he looks upon the Jews as a whole, scattered though they be over the face of the earth. My aim, however, has been to avoid any racial or religious limitations in the primary point of view chosen for the sifting of this question, and to look at many of the difficulties from the point of view of a thoroughly occidentalised and modernised Jew of

some Western country. I cannot judge how
far I have been able to maintain consistently
this point of view. I have thus also limited
my scope as regards the Jews themselves, in
every question which has actual practical bearings upon their life, to the educated citizens
fully established in our Western communities;
and my treatment is much more limited in
scope and restricted in its sphere of observation
than is that of the French savant.

On the other hand, this limitation may be
conducive to more exact results in a few definite instances, and it is from this side that I
would venture to criticise one or two features
in M. Leroy-Beaulieu's book, the whole of
which I so thoroughly and deeply appreciate
and admire.

The points in which I differ from M. Leroy-
Beaulieu are those contained in his two
chapters on the physiology and psychology of
the modern Jew. I even venture to believe
that some of his remarks will not bear close
analysis when compared with what he says in
these same chapters, and especially with what
he has said of the Jews in the other portions
of the book. I refer to his remarks on the
ideal position of conscience and honour in the

life of the modern Jew. The mistaken judgment which I believe he has there formed is,
to my mind, due to the very difference in the
standpoint which he has chosen to adopt in
his book, in contradistinction to the one which
I have endeavoured to hold in examining this
complex question.

The first of these misleading causes, in my
judgment, lies in the great width and diversity
of the people upon whom he is generalising.
He is really dealing with subtle and delicate
ideas, such as those of conscience and honour,
even in their most remote and delicate bearings on social life as they affect the most
developed stages of our Western civilised
intercourse, and here again (*hélas*) appealing
to a comparatively limited section of our own
communities. He is treating of the noblest
ideas of the noblest men and women among
us; and at the same time, as regards the Jews,
he is focussing so delicate a detail through the
endless horizon-line of the scattered Jewish
people all over the modern world, living under
conditions so diversified in their physical and
moral characteristics. But when dealing with
the characteristics of modern Occidental life,
the relation which the Jews hold to these

can only be fairly estimated in considering
those Jews whom, by origin and tradition, we
have called the Occidental Jew.   To allow the
Jews of Russia, Russian Poland, Galicia, the
Turkish empire, nay, even Africa, to come
into consideration while we are considering
these complex characteristics of essentially
Western civilisation lowers and vitiates, or, at
all events, confuses our just estimate of the
Western Jews' claims.   If we were studying,
for instance, the position which the Germans
of Slav origin in the German empire hold
with regard to some of the higher refinements
of German life, it would not add to the clearness of our investigation or the accuracy of
our results if we were to introduce at the
same time an estimate of the claims which the
serf-like Slav peasantry of Southern Russia
have to these qualities.   His own investigation in other portions of the book with regard
to the ethnology of the Jews living among us
agree with my own observations.   The Jews
of our Western States and nations, with whom
we are dealing in practical questions of our
modern life, have lived among us for many
ages and are essentially of us, only differing
individually among each other and from us as

we differ from one another, according to our
several conditions and occupations in life, and
the religious views and moral education which
each of us may have had instilled in youth.
And herein there is not so great a unity among
us, whatever our origin or the country we may
live in.   And when the broad characteristics
and ideals of our modern Occidental life are
discussed, I hold it to be radically wrong for a
Frenchman, or an Englishman, or a German, or
an American dealing with his fellow-countrymen of Jewish extraction in the light of such
questions, to use the pronoun 'they' at all.
It can only be a question of 'we.'   M. Leroy-
Beaulieu has mentioned individually a sufficient number of his own Jewish countrymen
of distinction, so varied in their talents, occupations, and tastes—but all of them true
Frenchmen ; and the same can be so readily
done for every other Western nation, that it
would be absurd for any practical purpose to
compare the ideals and conceptions of conscience and honour of these people with those
of a Jew of Smyrna, Cairo, or Morocco, and to
contrast the net result of such comparison with
our own local ideas on this subject.

The Jews of whom I am speaking have

come within the range of the same historical and national influences to which we have all been subjected in the formation of our characters—especially as regards our ideals of conscience and of honour. I will give one instance to illustrate my meaning.

I was once present at the discussion of the relation between England and the United States of America, and we were dwelling upon the changes in the popular feeling of Englishmen and Americans to one another. I was especially interested in the contribution of an American Jew to this discussion. He informed us of the struggle he had to undergo to overcome his national prejudice against the English. 'You see,' he said, 'my boyish days fell into the period of the American Civil War. My character with regard to patriotism and national prejudice received its stamp from this period (for it is no doubt in boyhood that one's character is formed in this respect), and, as there was a bitter feeling against England owing to the attitude of the English towards the North, I have since had much trouble in eradicating the influence of such lasting impressions of early life.' [1]

[1] M. Leroy-Beaulieu has given a similar instance of German patriotic prejudice on the part of a German Jew.

But I was especially interested in the picture which, at my request, he gave of his boyish life, and I venture to quote from it :—

'We were a large family of boys, and our life, when freed from our school work, had a definite war-like stamp. We were constantly playing at soldiers, building forts, fighting the rebels, and we were only too glad when we found real enemies in a set of rough street boys, who, jealous of our soldiers' uniforms and the forts we had built, ventured to attack us. The fight and the charges were really serious, as we tried to maintain the mock military discipline against the marauding host of stone-throwing roughs, and the result was broken heads and wounds which might have been grave. I believe we even delighted in the seriousness of our wounds as bringing us nearer to the bravery of real war. All through our boyish days our exploits on land and water were invigorating and not free from danger. We brothers were much attached to one another, and lived fairly at peace; but there was one word which invariably led to a fight, i.e. any doubt cast upon our conception of honour. We might call each other any name, heap opprobrium of any kind upon one another, it did not lead to blows; but one word mentioned was immediately and invariably followed by a blow straight from the shoulder; that word was " coward." '

I give this instance, not that it is remarkable, but as illustrating as well as any other the influence which a country and an age has in the formation of character. The character of this man was greatly influenced by the United States, and, moreover, the United States during the Civil War; and in so far it would differ from a character formed in the same country during a different period of its history. But this man was a Jew, and I venture to assert that thousands of Jews in Europe and America will find it to correspond in its essence to what moved them as boys.

The Western Jew has been influenced by the ideas of conscience and honour, which M. Taine ascribes to Christianity; they, as we all, have been nurtured by the Romantic spirit, beginning with Scott's novels—perhaps not always for the good. And it is absurd, in considering such ideas within the pale of our Western communities, to speak of the Western Jew as 'they' in lieu of 'we.'

Another point in which M. Leroy-Beaulieu

may have had his conclusions with regard to
the physiology and psychology of the Jews
slightly vitiated (though I heartily agree with,
and admire, most of what he says in these
chapters) is a matter of fact and history—
namely, the position which he assigns to the
Ghetto in the past life of the Jews—the
Ghetto as the symbol of misfortune and de-
basement.   In the first place, I believe that it
is a mistake to think that all the Jews lived
in the Ghetto.   The Ghetto did exist during
some periods in some of the capitals of the
mediæval world ; but the vast number of Jews,
dispersed about the country and living in
smaller towns, were not thus shut in.   I
should like to see this question carefully examined.   I have just received the genealogy
of a Jewish family, and among other things I
find that they lived in the self-same house in
a small German town (one of the most beautiful
houses of the town) continuously since 1680 ;
and I should say that many instances of this
kind might be found.   Furthermore, I believe
that the picture of the Ghetto as it exists in
the mind of most people, and even of M. Leroy-
Beaulieu, is an absolutely inaccurate one.   In
the first place, it is quite misleading to take

the Ghetto of Rome, Frankfort, or Venice, in
the aspect in which we of modern times have
seen them, as conveying any adequate idea of
what the Ghetto was when it really was a
Ghetto. Since the restrictions of habitation
have been raised from the Jews in these cities,
the better and more prosperous classes have all
left these quarters of the city. The result is
that they were filled merely with the refuse of
the Jewish plebs, who, like every other plebs,
will not impress us with the external dignity
of their life. I venture to believe that if we
could walk through the 'Juden Gasse' of
Frankfort, and perhaps even of Rome, of some
centuries ago, we should have been struck by
the comparative cleanliness and refinement,
perhaps even luxury, of the houses and of the
inhabitants.[1] I say comparative; and here
lies another point which must be remembered.
For we must not forget that the mediæval
cities (I am not speaking of the castles in the
country) differed vastly from our own in appearance, especially as regards cleanliness,
comfort, and hygienic arrangements. The
picture which we receive from authors and

---

[1] The house of the Jew of Lincoln, still standing, is one of
the most beautiful specimens of mediæval domestic architecture extant.

other sources of the traveller struggling through
the ill-paved, muddy, filthy streets of such a
city would lead me to find their parallel in the
Ghetto of Rome as it is to-day rather than in
the boulevards of modern Paris.

In many instances it might even be maintained that the houses of the Jews in those
days were the best and cleanest; and the life
within these houses probably corresponded to
this finer exterior. So, too, the influence of
the Ghetto may not have been as dangerous to
the formation of a sturdy character as we are
inclined to believe. I have more than once
insisted upon the fact that too much prominence has been given to the martyrology of
the Jews in its relation to their mediæval life
taken as a whole. The persecutions were few
and far between as regards each individual
district, and computed over a thousand years.
Every country suffered from warlike devasta-
tions and all that followed in its wake without
materially affecting the hereditary character of
the people. The physical life of the Jews
which lay between these periods of persecution corresponded, no doubt, in its fresh and
refined vitality, to the extant intellectual pro-
ducts which emanated from it. It is also a

mistake to believe that all the Jews, or any
great portion of them, in the Middle Ages,
came in contact, and had business, with
haughty and arrogant princes and nobles
before whom they had to bend their back,
and who crushed down their pride and manli-
ness. Most of the Jews really lived alone and
by themselves, and they had their own standards and their own pride, which were, on the
whole, of the nobler kind. The proportion of
those who had to bend their backs was smaller
than with the Christian nobility, among whom
there were many whose *whole life* was bound
up with such subserviency. For in the hier-
archy of the feudal world there was hardly one
man who had not to bend his back officially
before his superior. This is especially the case
with those in the immediate service of the
monarch, whose function may have been to
carry the platter, hand the cup, or hold the
shirt. And these personal offices were coupled
with the most pronounced symbols and customs of servility, and were the ground upon
which the elevation of most of the great noble
families of Europe rested, upon which their
distinction is based. They could not, however,
as could the Jew, after he had prostrated him-

self before the monarch with whose finances he
dealt, or, as a physician, held the pulse of the
decrepit representative of God on earth, prince
spiritual or secular—they could not, I say, return to their own quiet homes where there
existed for them spiritual standards of excellence independent of the approval of the
crowd without.   Such self-centredness, however, engenders true nobility of character.

I am willing to admit that, in many of its
important features, the idea of honour common to us all is to be traced back to mediæval
chivalry.   In one of its aspects it is the outcome of extreme individualism striving for the
glory of the individual as distinguished from
the mass of men ; it is aristocratic.   It is thus
an outcome of mediæval life and feudal times,
when each man fought by himself and lived in
his own castle.   And this side is knit up with
the whole conditions of feudal life in contradistinction to the life of the Greeks and
Romans, and the life of our modern society
with its ideal of humanitarianism.   Each man
then wished to excel, and there was established
a common code of moral and physical excellence.   Still, there was much of outer show, of
unreality, of *pour-la-galerie-dom*, of vulgarity

as a natural outcome of this spirit—it is the parent of all snobbishness. The Jew's life was generally spiritualised. His pride and honour, it is true, were generally not physical in character; but he had, and has, his honour, (*kofet*), his decency, his dignity, and his self-respect.

We must, however, always bear in mind that all these manifestations of virtue come from the same fountain-head—it is the overcoming of self-indulgence, in which the fear of pain is overpowered by the desire to do the right thing. The higher and more vivid the imagination and the power of realising consequences, the greater the demand upon courage. The outer manifestations differ according to the channels in which life flows; but the principle at the bottom is the same. And it is on this point that I am somewhat at issue with M. Leroy-Beaulieu. Whoever is possessed of moral courage can train himself into the performance of acts of physical courage; but it does not always hold good that he who possesses physical courage is proof in trials of moral valour. And if any weight is to be attached to general heredity as regards whole classes of people, then the Jew possesses the greatest claim to the heredity of these qualities, which, after all, give moral strength. If the following passage from M. Leroy-Beaulieu's book is accepted, the chances for the inheritance of spiritual refinement are in the Jew's favour. He says of them :—

'Beside the Jews the oldest of the old European nations are youthful. Which of our dynasties or of our feudal families would dare to compare the length of its years to that of the house of Israel? And we have here not only an antiquity of date. Israel is, above all, an ancient race by the antiquity of its culture. It is a long while (in Jerusalem, in Babylonia, in Alexandria) since for the sons of Jacob the work of the head and the hard labour of the brain have begun. If one wishes to consider the Jews as a race, here, perhaps, is the central point of importance : it is the most anciently cultured race of our Mediterranean world. While the civilisation of this race reaches furthest back, its culture has at the same time experienced least interruption. Twenty centuries are certainly a long duration for a human family. What, in this respect, are the inheritors of our ancient *bourgeoisie* and the sons of the Crusaders compared to the Levy's sons of the

Levites, and the numerous Cahen, Cohen, Kohn, Kahn, Coehn, whose well-authenticated ancestors, the cohanim of the Temple, burned incense before the Eternal on the altars of perfume, preparatory to going, in the shade of Babel, to discuss the origin of the world with the augurs of Chaldea and the magi of Iran?

'The antiquity and the continuity of their intellectual culture is (after their secular selection) that which, in my opinion, best explains the Jews and the place taken by Israel in our societies. They have come before us, they are our elder brothers. Their children learned to read in the rolls of the Thorah before our Latin alphabet was fixed—long before Cyril and Methodus had given an alphabet to the Slavs, before Runic inscriptions were known to the Germanic races of the North. Compared to them we are upstarts; they give us the lead in the matter of culture. Enclose them as much as we would for several hundred years behind the walls of the Ghetto, the day on which were torn the bars from their prison-gate, they had not much trouble in catching up with us—even on the roads which we had opened without them.'

As for their influence upon the idealism of

modern times, they can but strengthen its current. They have true idealism in their marrow, by which I mean the sacrifice of material desires to the preservation of an idea. I will venture to quote what I have myself said in the second chapter of this book : The martyrdom of the Jews is the most colossal instance of a steadfastness in a belief, in a great spiritual idea, to which all elements of life and all instincts of pleasure, and even self-preservation, are sacrificed. If this idealism is there, it is merely a matter of clear-sighted recognition in what channel its elevating power is to be turned. And I believe that the Jewish ideal for our future which M. Leroy-Beaulieu so beautifully depicts is one held by many (if not most) thoughtful people living within our Western civilisation ; it is the millennium of human love and fellowship, anti-romantic and anti-feudal in its character. As we have seen, the Middle Ages contained much that led to the worship of Mammon, to general snobbery, and anti-social instincts. The lowering and materialising of our ideals in modern times (which I believe holds good but for one small section or aspect of our modern life) is, as M. Leroy-Beaulieu has shown, in no way due to

the influence of the Jews, nor is it in part to
be ascribed to what he calls the 'American
spirit;' nor do I believe it to be due to what
he calls 'Neo-Paganism.' It springs from
numerous currents, all of which we cannot
attempt to enumerate here. But the main
causes are, on the one hand, the crumbling of
older standards, containing much that is essentially good, though they be insufficient for our
times ; and, on the other hand, the misdirected
currents of modern economical forces and institutions.

It is also a difficult matter to apply so delicate a term as conscience to a race, or even to a
nation. Conscience is a sense of abstract duty
developed into a moral faculty, which guides
and judges our actions. It is called into activity
to enable us to estimate the gap between our
actual life and our ideal life. The Jews have
had this sense of duty to the highest degree ;
not so much the Biblical Jews as the mediæval
and modern Jews. They may not always have
turned it into definite social channels, they may
not have contributed as much to the refinement of our social conscience as they did to
our broader moral conscience ; but this is an
historical accident.

Practical conscience, we will find in looking about us, is not so much a matter of race and racial inheritance as it is a matter of tradition within the various vocations. Certain trades and professions have developed their own standards of right and wrong—some higher, some lower: horse-dealing, art-dealing, publishing have in some countries and ages developed different standards of honesty from other trades, and so in the many other walks of life. The occupations of the Jews present the greatest variety now, and in the past, as we have seen, they have been accidental and not essential to the inner nature of that people. But what is not accidental and not vacillating is the initial sense of abstract duty, the vitality of conscience; and with regard to these the conditions of Jewish life have ever been most favourable.

Honour is practical conscience, conscience carried into action ; and the man of honour is one in whom this practical conscience has become second nature, an ineradicable habit. But we must all realise how frequent are the changes in the denotation of this term *honour*. Each period and every country has its peculiar conception of it, and the one age may oppose

X

or ridicule the conception held by another, as one country may deny the code of its neighbour. One country may consider it to be a stern dictate of the code of honour to fight a duel in satisfaction of wounded vanity; while another country may laugh it away. But what always remains, and will remain, is the connotation of honour—the practical conscience as affecting our common social life, so effective that we are prepared to give up our lives in order to follow its dictates. The Jews have constantly and continuously made this sacrifice for things spiritual which they valued highly.

And now let us examine the subtler and more delicate developments of such principles in the lighter aspects of our social life, the question of the *parvenu*. It is true that many Jews have 'worked their way up;' but it has not been so great a step for them to make, as I have endeavoured to show in the third chapter. The Jewish *parvenu* and the Christian *parvenu* are very different things, because the Jews have had a standard of their own, and one which was not compared to others and then considered second-rate. They may have been foreigners to the great social world; but

as such they have never had to unlearn the
habit of dropping h's; in so far they have
started unhampered. But, on the other hand,
they have inherited that inner refinement
which the poor 'Talmud-yude' was possessed
of as a Jew. They were not illiterate to start
with, nor had they to shed the thick skin
of coarseness; but, as M. Leroy-Beaulieu has
put it, 'they are the most anciently cultured
race.'

But let us look about us in European and
American society, and where do we not find
the *parvenu*? Do you require many generations of continuous affluence and conditions of
cultured life? I believe that in Europe, as
well as in America, you would find it hard to
discover a society which is for the greater part
made up of members who could point to
circumstances under which the conditions of
repose, of affluence, and of leisure, acting
during many generations and continuously,
had so affected the organic life of the family
as to enable one generation to transmit to the
other, even as a tradition, the higher qualities.

What does *le monde* mean when applied to
modern European societies, except when we
meet with it in old-fashioned novels? Does

this *world* really exist so that we can define it accurately, and point at it with our fingers ?

I believe it does not. The old *monde* is completely disorganised, owing to many causes: First, there is the dying out of the feudal spirit, and the clear-cut limitations which it gave. And I even doubt whether, according to our present notions, feudalism by itself could create a distinguished *monde* ; for, besides its inherent dangers in tending towards snobbishness, it required the centre of a court and a metropolis for the formation of *salons* where some distinction and refinement might be infused into the country squire and the *Land-junker*. Furthermore, the economical changes since the French Revolution have shifted the spheres of wealth and prosperity. An impoverished Faubourg Saint-Germain becomes ridiculously assertive, and approaches dangerously near to the shabby-genteel. And, finally, our centres of life have become too large. The capitals of Europe have not one society, one *monde*, but a great many. Moreover, the best, the most refined, the most ' *homme-du-mondish*,' are not always those sets which are grossly and manifestly so. I believe my experience will be borne out in looking into the *monde* of the European

capitals, perhaps even of America, that those
sets which are socially most well-bred are not
always, and perhaps not even generally, found
among those which are on the face of it the
leaders of society.   This was, perhaps, not the
case in former years.   Though in those days
the educated *bourgeois* might claim certain
moral and intellectual qualities as being
especially his own, he would admit that in the
social refinement of manners, in physical grace,
in tact and all that it means, the gentleman, the
nobleman, or cavalier of his day was superior
to him.   But now, can we truthfully say that
this is the case?   The interests of the stock-
exchange (not owing to the defilement of the
individual intruders from that body, whether
Jews or Gentiles) have crept into the minds
and have left a stamp upon the manners and
the tone of intercourse.   The newspapers,
especially the society papers, and the vulgar
publicity to which they lead, have introduced
that self-consciousness which we ascribe to the
most pronounced *parvenu*.   The intercourse
with grooms and jockeys have converted the
knight who rode his horse in the tourney with
some idea of risk, into a swaggering loiterer in
stables and on race-courses, with the stupidity
of a jockey, the acumen of a book-maker, and

the market-place vanity of a *garçon coiffeur*. What manners or grace of bearing have many of the *jeunesse dorée* of London, Paris, Berlin, Vienna, or Newport? Awkward and stupidly shy, if not coarse and swaggering. Illiterate and gross in taste, selling libraries and works of art which their ancestors have collected, and looking upon the refined Jew or merchant who buys them for his house as a *parvenu* or an outsider. And many of the recognised circles of highest social life in the European capitals, what is their aggregate tone? After all, if we are truthful, how *bourgeois*, how provincial, they are; how dependent upon their surroundings and the standards of their own material life! The *homme du monde* is, after all, he who has seen the world, as opposed to the provincial and the *épicier*; who is at home in all sets and is always above each; who conforms, but is not held by the narrow codes, knowing the wider circles; who is tolerant, because he knows how relative all these views are.

Now, the best tone, the best manners, the most refined *salons* are in most capitals found in sets that (fortunately for them) are not noticed in society papers; but one has met with social refinement in families that are not known to the outer world and shrink from it, and one has often found this in Jewish families.

I would ask the question, how many gentlemen and gentlewomen among the hundreds, perhaps thousands, whom we have met claiming these epithets will stand all the tests on the long-run? How many who have inner nobility and refinement of taste with outer grace of demeanour, considerateness, and tact; whose intellectual education embraces, at least as regards their sympathies, all the varied spheres of noble mental effort; whose moral culture is so deep and true that they can afford to be light and tolerant on the surface of social conduct without calling in the need of the force-pumps, bucketing up priggishness from the heavy deposit of principles at the bottom of their conscience; whose nature is strung so that all the notes are true in tone; from whom we have never received a jar from their blank limitation or from tortuous mal-formation of taste, from meanness or grossness —a sudden disappointment or shock to the best cravings within us putting us out of tune for a whole day, like an ugly picture or a discordant sound? How many have you met, of whatever class of society you may think?

And the wrestling for distinction and display pointed out by M. Leroy-Beaulieu, the grossness of the *parvenu* he refers to, have you not found some, if not all of them, among your closest friends of the highest social distinction? They may sometimes be found among dukes and nobles whose ancestors go back to the crusaders, and among princes of the blood. Thackeray has seen them and has immortalised them. An act such as the attempt to write a book defending a people from abuse, as has been written by M. Leroy-Beaulieu, the tone of fairness, refinement, and depth of sympathy with which it is pervaded, brings me nearer in mind to the picture of a true gentleman, *sans peur et sans reproche*, than many a glaring act of valour, or a life passed among the most refined brilliancy of modern social life.

A gentleman is, after all, as has so often been said, made by the kindness of the heart, the tenderness within strength, the *alma gentil.* Tact is the rapid and true action directed by ready sympathy, which keeps us from saying or doing what will harm or cause discomfort to our neighbours—it is lovingkindness and unselfishness carried into our slightest actions. Having these, any man may become a gentleman in any sense. Failing these, he will never be a true gentleman, however favourable the circumstances. But with them and with intellectual refinement and culture, put a boy into noble social surroundings, and he will become an ornament to every *salon* into which he steps. But take care that you do not remind him of the fact that he is tolerated!

Here lies the difficulty. No man can display these social qualities, nor can he avoid some appearance of snobbishness, if by your action you make the social ground upon which he stands and moves unsteady, and rob him of the grace and lightness of intercourse. He will be bound to become assertive in some direction and deprived of his social ease. The Jews of Paris, Berlin, and London had refined *salons* a hundred years ago, and many of them were, and are, ornaments to any society; but remind them of their exceptional position, let them realise that, however absurd and unjust, the basis upon which they stand is doubtful, and you will produce a consciousness which will lead to assertion, and to a sensitiveness and reticence which act almost in the same way, 'How often are we thought proud and arrogant,' I was told by a Jew, ' when we retire and refuse to join in with the others! But can we be treated as exceptions with a super-

Y

added patronising affability on the part of our social equals who make this exception?'

I believe M. Leroy-Beaulieu was wrong when he spoke of his Jewish compatriots as 'they,' even to praise them. What must the feelings of his Jewish friends be when he dwells upon the high spiritual quality of the Jew, prefacing it by '*ce petit juif!*' How would he like an Englishman to dwell upon a whole catalogue of French virtues in assuring the world that 'that little Frenchman has, after all, conferred the greatest boon upon humanity through his French Revolution,' etc.?

No, leave your Jewish compatriots alone, and you will be astonished at the number of cultured and refined men and women among them.

They exist, those gentlemen and gentle-women possessed of noble, generous, and brave hearts, with refined feelings, guided by wide minds, and all attuned into harmony by natural grace of manner; they exist, but singly, not in masses. They are scattered through all nations and sets, they form a great international society.

The wider our circle of humanity, the more active our social feeling, the more individual must our judgment of man become for 'social' purposes. We do not admit people into our circles in classes or tribes, nor should we choose this method of exclusion. The Occidental Jew must be dealt with individually, as an ordinary member of the community among which he lives. If any virtue which he possesses has come to him by racial heredity, this will be to his advantage, and is for him a matter of his inner consciousness, to remember this with a feeling of piety towards his progenitors.

But I have been doubting, while writing this book and while reading M. Leroy-Beaulieu's work, whether in common with many modern authors in other domains, we have not been exaggerating the importance of heredity? The newness of the discovery in the natural and medical sciences has, as is not unfrequently the case, led to a premature application of these delicate results of theory to the complicated body of practical social phenomena. It is not easy to gauge the result of racial heredity in the mind and character, the actions and general deportment of individuals. In such an attempt we may make many a blunder. And, after all, what is the gain of such speculation? But what we do realise more and more in studying nations and social communities is the force of tradition and the manner in which it is handed down. These traditions have lasting power and vitality, and it is our duty to select from them—to confirm, support, and to increase the vitality of those that are good, and to counter-act, and, if possible, extirpate, those that are bad.

And when we think of the Jews, we must admit the great truth which M. Leroy-Beaulieu has so forcibly put : that their virtues are their own, their vices are our making. Their virtues are the result of Judaic teaching and the elements essential to Judaism : their vices are the result of circumstances which the mediæval world massed about their life. It is our duty to clear away this mass of vicious circumstance, and to give free play to the inherent, righteous vigour of this, the most ancient of cultured peoples.

Printed by T. and A. CONSTABLE, Printers to Her Majesty at the Edinburgh University Press

Gay and Bird's

Publications

LONDON: 5, CHANDOS STREET, STRAND

INDEX.